The Mystery of the
Vikings in America

The Mystery of the Vikings in America

Morton J. Golding

J. B. LIPPINCOTT COMPANY
Philadelphia and New York

Picture Sources

Pages 18, 41, 46: Swedish Information Service. Pages 33, 34: Museum of National Antiquities, Stockholm. Pages 39, 73, 92: Nordisk Pressefoto A/S. Pages 45, 75: Danish National Museum. Pages 48, 49, 50: Copyright Universitetets Oldsaksamling, Oslo. Page 54: Swedish National Tourist Office, New York. Pages 52, 104, 105: reproduced from the collections of the Library of Congress. Pages 38, 39, 42, 55: New York Public Library Picture Collection. Pages 77, 78, 82, 83, 103, 120–121: reprint from "The Norsemen in Greenland," Danish Foreign Office Journal Number 58–1967. Published by the Danish Ministry of Foreign Affairs. Pages 86–87: Yale University Press. Pages 109, 110: photo provided through the courtesy of the Newfoundland and Labrador Tourist Development Office, St. John's. Page 141: Newport County Chamber of Commerce, Newport, Rhode Island, and Rhode Island Development Council. Page 145: State of Minnesota, Department of Economic Development.

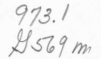

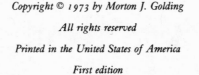

U.S. Library of Congress Cataloging in Publication Data

Golding, Morton J
 The mystery of the Vikings in America.

 SUMMARY: Explores available clues and evidence that the Vikings were the first discoverers of America.
 1. America—Discovery and exploration—Norse—Juvenile literature. 2. Vikings—Juvenile literature.
 [1. America—Discovery and exploration—Norse. 2. Vikings] I. Title.
 E105.G56   973.1'3   73-4541
 ISBN-0-397-31247-4

For my sons—

Geoffrey and Gower

And, of course,

For Pat

Contents

Introduction

___

When we see Vikings in adventure films and read about them in novels, they are usually portrayed as a warrior race of tall, clean-cut men and beautiful women who set out to discover America for the sheer fun of it.

What were they really like, those men and women whom story-tellers place in America long before Columbus arrived? Did they truly come to this continent? And, if they did, how did they act, live, fight, make love? What sort of people were they to come here in the first place?

They were here, all right. The evidence, as I shall show in this book, is all but overwhelming. But a good deal about them remains unknown. To an amazingly large extent, the Vikings are a mystery.

Nor will I pretend to have cleared the mystery up. No one, short of some science-fiction time-traveler, could accomplish that. Too many centuries have passed since the Vikings lived. The records concerning them are too skimpy and filled with too many contradictions.

Yet, there are facts. There are clues. What this book is meant to do is to give the facts and present the clues. Once you have them—once you have the known facts and the suppositions and the reasons for the suppositions—you can draw your own conclusions as to what lies behind the Viking story.

This is a kind of mystery, in other words. But one in which *you* will have to play the role of super-sleuth detective.

In the words of Ellery Queen, the reader is challenged.

The Mystery of the
Vikings in America

I.

To Be a Viking

Volumes far thicker than this could be written about what we do not know about the Vikings. Much about them and their way of life remains a mystery—even the origin of the name "Viking" itself.

Most scholars agree that this name did not originate with the Scandinavians, but with their victims—those peoples whose villages, castles, and monasteries were raided by them. The victims may have borrowed the Old Norse word *vikingr*, which meant pirate. Since the Vikings were certainly considered pirates by those whom they raided, this explanation has a great deal of logic to it. And it is also true that Old English sources from the ninth century referred to the Norse as *wicingas*, a word which appears to have been used for both pirate and sailor.

But there are other explanations. One is that "Viking" came from an Old English word, *wic*, which meant encampment. Since the building of temporary camps was a common practice among raiding Vikings, this idea, too, seems logical.

Still another theory states that "Viking" is derived from the Old

Norse *vic,* which means creek or inlet. Proponents of this view point out that the Viking raiders hugged the shoreline and made good use of both creeks and inlets. But no agreement on how the Vikings got their name has yet been reached.

This, as we shall see, is what happens over and over in discussing the Vikings. Informed guess follows informed guess, but we still have to make up our own minds and take our choice.

No matter what the true origin of the name "Viking" may have been, the Vikings did exist. And we can be sure of certain facts about them.

The Vikings were the last of a whole succession of raiders and conquerors who came down from the Northlands. In fact, their early ancestors overran Europe and helped destroy the mighty Roman Empire.

The ancestors of the Vikings lived in tribes. They called themselves simply "the People," or—in their own language—*Theut.* It is from that word, *Theut,* that we get our contemporary terms, Teuton and *Deutsch* and Dutch.

None of the old tribes kept written records. The only written accounts of them we have come from their enemies.

The most famous of these accounts was done by a Roman writer, Tacitus. In A.D. 98—during the greatest days of the Empire—Tacitus wrote a book called *Germania,* which presents the most detailed description of the Germanic tribes now available.

As far as anyone today can tell, Tacitus himself never met a Teuton. He interviewed Roman soldiers and officials who did come into contact with them, and based his book on what they said.

Tacitus admired the Germanic "barbarians" in the same way that many a nineteenth-century writer admired the American Indian "barbarians," for their primitive virtues.

The Germans, he tells us, were a free and noble people. The men were great warriors and fierce fighters. The women—in contrast to the free-thinking Roman women of Tacitus' day—were highly moral and obedient.

Despite Tacitus' habit of romanticizing the tribesmen—and his implicit insult, calling them "noble savages"—his work remains our fullest and most reliable source of information. Anyone who is interested in getting a vivid picture of the Germanic tribes should read a translation of *Germania*.

There are other sources, naturally. These include discussions by other Roman writers, archaeological evidence from Scandinavia and lands through which the tribes wandered, the Germanic law-codes and the Teutonic epic poems such as the fierce and bloody British epic, *Beowulf*.

The last of the Germanic invaders, the Vikings began their era of conquest around A.D. 850. The original Germanic wanderings began almost nineteen hundred years before that—around 1000 B.C.

Some historians believe that the migrations came about as a result of warfare between the tribes in Scandinavia. Tacitus mentioned a tendency toward intertribal warfare as a fatal weakness of the Germans of his day, and said that they would be a far greater danger to Rome if they should unite.

We must keep in mind that Tacitus was writing more than a millennium after the first migrations began, and it is always risky to assume that a people's life-style has remained consistent over such a long period of time. But *if* such warfare were common in early Scandinavia, it is more than likely that the losers would have been forced out of their territories and would wander southward (where else can you wander from Scandinavia?) in search of new ones.

Another theory holds that the migrations were caused by a population explosion in the north. If the food supply could not keep up with population growth, some tribes would obviously have had to go.

Nothing is yet known about the first nine hundred years of the

Norsemen's wanderings. It was not until the tribesmen crossed the river Rhine and faced forces of the Roman Empire that accounts of them were written down.

The first encounter, which came in 100 B.C., must have been a great shock to both sides. Before this, the tribesmen had only to deal with peace-loving Celtic farmers whom they bullied pretty much at will. Now they were up against the well-trained armies of Rome.

It was the legions of Julius Caesar who finally defeated the tribesmen and pushed them back across the Rhine. But the Teutons refused to give up. Attracted by the riches of Rome, they tried over and over again to invade what was then called Gaul. With the exception of one temporary success in the middle of the third century A.D., however, they were kept on the other side of the Rhine until the final collapse of that Roman frontier in the year 406.

The story of the decline of the Roman Empire, its slow crumbling before the invading "barbarians," and the gradual civilizing of the "barbarians"—who became the forerunners of modern Europe—has been told many times and in many ways. It is the history of the birth of the Middle Ages, as well as the history of the death of Rome.

However fascinating that story is, though, we are more concerned with the descendants of the early tribesmen who stayed home in Scandinavia. For it was just those descendants who were to develop into the Vikings.

Among the last of the original Teutonic invasions were those carried out in the fifth and sixth centuries by Angles, Saxons, Jutes, and other tribesmen who invaded the British Isles. For some two hundred years after that final expansion, Scandinavia appeared to have settled down.

But appearances can be deceptive. There must have been a hidden rumbling somewhere below the apparently peaceful surface, a rumbling which, in the ninth century, was to erupt into the Viking era.

The great age of Viking conquest and exploration began in the ninth century and continued into the eleventh. During that time, the Vikings were probably the greatest sailors, shrewdest merchants, and fiercest soldiers in the world. Even after Viking conquest finally ceased, the Vikings' successors in Scandinavia remained forces to be reckoned with.

As sailors, the Vikings set forth in vessels that were masterpieces of the shipbuilder's art. They ranged far to the south, the east, and the west. They did not necessarily sail in order to raid or to wage war. Often they went out on pure trading voyages. But if they were attacked, they usually won, and when they traded, they usually got the best of the bargain.

In their excursions to the east, the Vikings ranged throughout the Baltic Sea. They established trading stations along the shore, and sent their raiders deep into what is now Russia.

The most famous of the Viking tribes that invaded Russia was the Rus—a Swedish group which gave that country its modern name. In Sweden, the Rus had a reputation for piracy. They arrived in Russia during the first part of the ninth century, and within a hundred years gained control of many centers from Novgorod in the north to Kiev in the south.

Vikings also struck out along the Atlantic coast of Europe and the British Isles. In England they battled the descendants of the earlier Teutonic invaders and managed to dominate much of that country for nearly two centuries. In France they took over an entire province, which was then renamed Normandy after the men from the north.

From their new home in Normandy, the Vikings, now called Normans, began a series of still more far-flung raids and conquests. They penetrated the Mediterranean Sea and conquered the Arab-controlled island of Sicily in the year 1060. They were still engaged in quelling resistance there when they started their conquest of England in 1066. Eventually these men from the north who had settled in France would found dynasties in both England and Sicily.

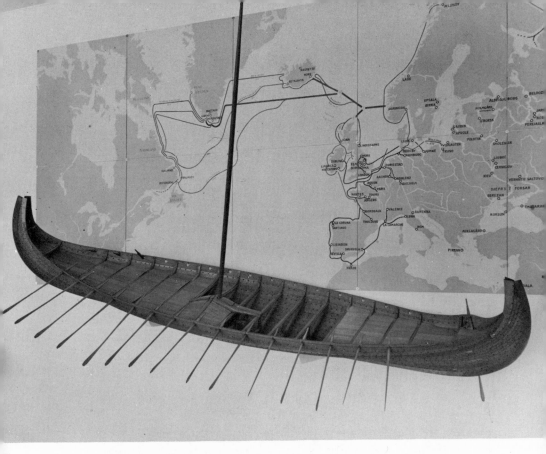

Model of a big Norwegian Viking ship used in the ninth, tenth, and eleventh centuries. Above the ship, a map showing the Viking expeditions during that time. While the Norsemen sailed mainly westward and the Danes west and southward, the Swedish Vikings followed the big Russian rivers down to the Black Sea and far into the Mediterranean.

Vikings raided in Spain, too, and in the northern sections of Africa. A short-lived Viking kingdom, in fact, was apparently set up in what is now Morocco.

But what manner of men and women were these Vikings? What must it have been like to have lived in the Scandinavia of A.D. 800 to 1000?

First of all, it would have meant being born into a world of dark and brutal winters only briefly relieved by a summer that was all too short. For some mysterious reason, the Northlands were growing colder at the beginning of the Viking era. A farm that was just managing to hold its own in the Scandinavian highlands during the seventh century A.D., for instance, might have had to be abandoned during the ninth. The ever more frigid climate could make an already hard-to-work farm impossible.

This was a harsh and rugged world, which bred a harsh and rugged people. In Viking Scandinavia, only the strong were equipped to survive.

Under these conditions, we might expect the Vikings to have made good use of their heritage from Teutonic times. And so they did. During the two centuries that had elapsed between the last of the Teutonic invasions and the start of the Viking era, few changes, if any, had taken place in the northern way of life. Customs had remained essentially the same.

What does all this mean?

It means that if you were a Viking boy, for example, you would have been trained from earliest childhood to battle fiercely for all that belonged to you. As a very little boy, you would have been taken out of the hands of your mother and trained by the men of the house to be proud and warlike and never to let anyone deny your rights or take anything away from you.

An extreme example of the kind of boy the Northlands produced comes from the saga of Egil Skallagrimsson, who was a tenth-century Viking hero. When Egil was twelve he was punished sternly by his father. Normally, Egil might have accepted the punishment, but in this case he thought it was unfair. The only way he could salve his pride was to take revenge. Egil's method? That very night, he crept up behind his father's most valuable serf—his chief overseer—and killed him.

A horrifying and disgusting story? To us it is. But not to the Vikings.

"What better way for Egil to have taken revenge," an imaginary Viking might ask, "than to have destroyed his father's property?"

"But that was murder," we might reply with indignation. "And a cowardly murder at that! To sneak up behind a man and kill him in the dark. . . ."

But by now our imaginary Viking might well be puzzled.

"What *man?*" he would demand. "What *man* did Egil kill?"

"Why, the serf. The chief overseer."

"But a serf is not a man. He is a piece of property—like a goat or a bull calf is a piece of property. Would you call Egil a coward if he'd crept up behind a goat in order to kill him in safety?"

At this stage the dialogue would have to break down. We are talking from two different ages with completely different points of view.

The Vikings honestly believed that serfs were not human. It is a belief, incidentally, that many early societies had. Even the highly "civilized" Greeks and Romans would have understood the Viking position far more easily than they would have understood our own.

We, of course, cannot accept the Viking point of view. But if we want a lifelike picture of the Vikings we will have to hold our moral judgments in abeyance and remember that the Vikings were not only different from us, but were living in a far more difficult and primitive time.

Egil's father—a Viking—did accept his son's act. He did not punish the boy. He let the incident drop. He was probably rather proud of his son's act in standing up for his rights.

Viking boys received training in arms and warfare. Viking girls did not. It was the males who were expected to do the fighting when they grew up, while the females had children and took care of domestic chores.

Norse women, however (that is, the free women, not the female serfs), were highly respected. They were probably more liberated, in the modern sense, than any other women of their time. A Viking woman, for example, would not dream of taking her husband's name simply because she married him. This practice continued in Scandinavia until the eighteenth century.

Women were not considered to be delicate, mindless creatures. When a man was off on a long sea voyage, it was up to his wife to run the farm and control the rough male serfs. If a band of armed marauders attacked the farm—as all too often happened during this period—she would have to organize the defense. On some occasions she did arm herself and join in the battle.

A free Viking woman did not plead for respect. She demanded it. And heaven help the man who refused to give it to her. A good illustration of this can be found in the tale of a Norse lady named Hallgärd.

Hallgärd was married to a man named Gunnar, who once made the error of boxing her ears. She was not physically strong enough to prevent this indignity. But neither would she accept it. She bore the insult grimly and waited her chance.

This came some time later when the couple were away from their home and allies. A group of Gunnar's enemies surrounded them and the man was forced to defend himself with bow and arrow. Gunnar was a good bowman and more than held his own until his bowstring began to fray. At that point he turned to Hallgärd and asked her to cut some of her hair to weave an emergency bowstring.

But Hallgärd made no move to comply.

"Do you remember the time that you boxed my ears?" she asked sweetly. "Well, now I don't care whether you are able to defend yourself or not."

It took a while but, according to the story, Gunnar's bowstring finally snapped and he was killed.

Whether this tale is truth or fiction, it does point up the tremendous pride in themselves that the Viking women had. Stories and poems of long-suffering wives who meekly bore their husbands' abuse come from many cultures. But none that I know of come from the Vikings in Scandinavia.

Among such people, what we term "romantic love" would seem to have been out of place. And so it was. Courting couples did not listen to songs of love while they held hands in the moonlight. As a matter of fact, love songs were banned as harmful during the entire Viking era.

As for marriage, that was looked upon as too serious a matter to be left to the whims and desires of youth. Marriage was a business proposition—something to be arranged by parents for the mutual advantage of the respective families.

Strong bonds of affection did grow up between husbands and wives, of course. And since those bonds grew out of mutual respect for each other as people rather than as romantic objects, it is probable that married love was at least as strong then as it is today.

The strongest love in a Viking's life, however, was his family: not just his children and his spouse, but his parents, his siblings, and his siblings' spouses. Those were the people to whom he was closest and most loyal. The basic pattern of the early Teutons repeated itself during Viking times. The family came first.

Next to the family, as in Teutonic days, came the clan—more distant relatives who lived nearby and who could be relied upon for aid in time of need. As for strangers and outsiders, they might be dealt with in a peaceable fashion, but were usually kept at a safe distance unless they married into the clan.

In this family- and clan-oriented world, the greatest single bond of all was between father and son. A Viking father thought of his son as representing his future and the future of his line. A son was living proof that a man's honor and manhood need not die with him.

It was the son's obligation—and one which he undertook eagerly —to safeguard his father's honor. He took on the quarrels of his father. If an elder Viking was killed in a fight, he could die secure in the knowledge that his son would avenge him. This philosophy of honor and vengeance produced blood feuds that could last for generations.

The greatest tragedy that could befall a Viking, therefore, was the death of a favorite son. When this happened, it was as if the Viking's world had come to an end.

We have already taken a look at the story of the Viking boy-hero, Egil Skallagrimsson. Later, when Egil had become a man, he suffered the agony of losing his favorite son.

Egil's reaction to this was deeply Viking. He did not shake his fist at the heavens or rant at fate. He simply shut himself up in his room and refused to eat so that he might starve himself to death. The fact that Egil did not starve was due to another child: his wise and loving daughter, Thorgerd.

After Egil had gone without food for some time, Thorgerd begged to be allowed to keep him company. If her father wished to die, she said, she had no wish to live either.

After some discussion, Egil agreed. Father and daughter sat together, apparently waiting for the end. Finally a servant came with an oxhorn of water. If they would not eat, at least they could quench their thirst.

Thorgerd drank first, then handed the oxhorn to Egil. He took several deep gulps before he realized how he had been tricked. Instead of water, the horn contained nourishing milk.

Now Thorgerd faced her father boldly and told him that this should mark the end of their plan of mutual starvation. She challenged him to live on and write a great elegy—a memorial poem—in honor of her dead brother.

Egil agreed. The poem still exists, and is one of the finest examples of Old Norse poetry.

We can see, then, that the "savage" Vikings were not devoid of the nobler emotions. If a Viking's anger could be terrible, his love could be strong and tender.

The Vikings were no more all of a piece than we ourselves are. The more we know about them, the more we will find them contradictory. For every fact about them that we find to abhor, we will find a fact to admire.

The only generalization we can make about their character is that it seemed to run to extremes. The Vikings—unlike some philosophers of the Greeks and Romans—never considered the "golden mean," or moderate path, something to admire.

But what of the wider world in which the Vikings lived? How did they relate to other peoples? What of their religion and politics?

II.

The Soil, the Sea, and the Gods

Viking farmers were a self-sufficient breed. Unlike modern American farmers, they could find just about everything they needed to live right on their own land. Farm families not only raised their own food crops and bred their own livestock, but produced their own clothing and even built smithies in order to smelt iron and cast bronze for implements and weapons.

Even after death, a Norseman's land would have its role to play. Two fields were invariably set aside as burial plots—one for the family, the other for the slaves and serfs.

The difference between serfs and slaves is not always clear. Slaves were normally non-Scandinavians. People of any status could be ripped away from their homes and made slaves, if they were unlucky enough to be captured in Viking raids. Serfs, on the other hand, lived under a form of "modified" slavery. They had been born on the land, belonged to it, and could expect to die on it. It might be assumed that it was not as difficult being a serf as being a slave.

Despite the self-sufficiency of their lives, farmers were not entirely cut off from the outside world. Wandering craftsmen—men-of-all-work—traveled from farm to farm, visiting the farmers and selling their own special skills.

In his oaken tool chest, a handyman could carry equipment for any specialized types of jobs. He was both a carpenter and a metalworker. He could manufacture items ranging from spear shafts to iron nails. Any skilled work which a farmer was not able or did not wish to do for himself, a craftsman could do for him.

But the handymen undoubtedly had another function as well. They were the ones who must have passed along gossip and news from farm to farm, letting the farmers know who got married, who died, who had gone off to war. In a time before newspapers or television commentators, the wandering craftsmen took on the functions of both.

Even in the early days, however, all Scandinavians did not either live on farms or wander between them. There were also settlements and military camps where people lived together both for mutual defense and for purposes of trade.

Trade seems to have been the prime force behind most of the Scandinavian towns which developed during the Viking era. In addition to their background as farmers and their reputation as warriors and pirates, the Norsemen were master traders. Their merchants, indeed, were probably the most successful of their day.

Before the start of the Viking period, much of Scandinavia's foreign trade was handled by a people called the Frisians whose territory was centered near the mouth of the Rhine in what is now Holland. The Frisians were a seafaring people who grew prosperous during the eighth and ninth centuries by playing the role of honest broker between Scandinavia on the one hand and the Mediterranean lands on the other.

All this was very good for the Frisians, but the Norsemen were not the sort to enjoy being dependent on others. Soon they began designing their own ships, which—as we shall see in the next chapter—were vast improvements over all that had come before. While the Frisians were fine merchants and good seamen, it was their bad luck to come up against a people who were to develop into even better merchants and perhaps the finest seamen in the history of the world.

Norse merchant seamen fell into two basic categories: those who worked at this trade full time and those who did so only half of the time.

The full-time seaman spent his life with his ship. In winter, he would lay his vessel up at whatever port he happened to be in, and load new supplies on board during the spring in order to take them back to Scandinavia when the thaw set in.

The second sort of merchant was only partly dependent on his ship. He would also have his own estate which his family, serfs, and slaves would work while he was off on a trading voyage. It was this second type of seaman-farmer who helped to develop the Norse market towns.

Such a town would attract merchants from all over a general area. It was the natural place for farmers to sell their own products in exchange for spices, glassware, and other luxury items produced in the non-Scandinavian world.

One important early market town was Haithabu (now Hedeby in West Germany) which was located in the southern section of the Danish peninsula of Jutland. Haithabu got a boost to prominence as the result of a Norse raid on another trading town, Reric, which belonged to a Slavic tribe, the Obotrites. The Norse removed all the merchants from Reric (probably located near the present-day city of Rostock on the Baltic Sea) and transported them in a body to Haithabu.

The raid on Reric was carried out in 808 by King Godfred of Denmark. Afterwards, still more merchants came to Haithabu—this time on their own. This fresh supply of merchants included Norsemen, but was not limited to them. Saxon and Frisian tradespeople now realized that they could live and trade peacefully in Haithabu and were drawn there in search of profits.

Haithabu began life as a small town. As the years passed, however, it grew into an important trading center with homes, warehouses, and workshops. Its facilities were used to ship goods from the south to the more northerly sections of Scandinavia.

The growth of Haithabu and other towns like it was dependent on peaceful conditions. While trade can overcome many obstacles, it rarely flourishes in places where merchants are in constant fear of having their warehouses broken into and their property and possessions destroyed. So although the Vikings would raid foreign nations whenever they chose, they had to protect the Norse market towns from both home-grown bandits and foreign raiders. This meant that there had to be a strong central government—some force that was powerful enough to make the rules and keep the peace. And, at the time we are talking about, that meant a monarchy.

It should come as no surprise, therefore, to find that the power of the early Norse kings was apparently centered in the towns. Rural Scandinavians—clannish, family-centered, and comparatively isolated and self-sufficient—were far less easily controlled than the merchants, who were more dependent on the king's keeping the peace. Although farmers and large landowners fought for their king in time of war, their first loyalties seemed to lie with their clan, their families, and their own sense of honor. There are, in fact, many records telling of family feuds between Viking lords and their kings.

In the towns it was another matter. A king would bring merchants and artisans together, lay down a strong set of laws to insure their safety, and then set up a system of taxation. It was through the money collected by this taxation that the power of the Norse kings gradually increased.

The names of the three great Viking kingdoms—those of the Swedes, the Danes, and the Norwegians (the Finns were not Vikings nor, properly speaking, Scandinavians)—are still familiar to us today. The territory they occupied differed somewhat from the modern nations of Sweden, Denmark, and Norway, but not so much as to be unrecognizable. When you look at a map of Scandinavia in Viking times, you'll have no trouble recognizing the different kingdoms.

When and how did the kingdoms become unified? The answer differs from country to country.

Sweden is the country whose history we know least about. For while archaeological finds in Sweden date back thousands of years B.C., archaeologists have found no written historical information from before about A.D. 1000. The nation was apparently unified during the seventh century. But just how the process took place, no one can truly say.

It is known that the Swedes concentrated most of their Viking activities in the east. Although they did carry out a number of raids

Europe at the beginning of the Viking era.

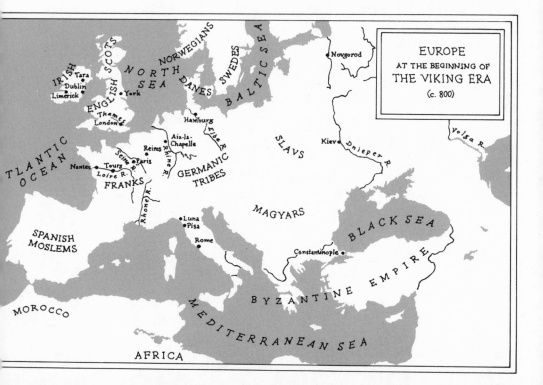

to the south and even raided Denmark itself, they never went "Westviking" across the Atlantic. The Danes and the Norwegians did, however. It is fortunate that we know more about them, because they (especially the Norwegians) brought their cultural heritage to Europe and the New World.

We know something more about early political life in Denmark.

The most important of the early Danish kings was Godfred—the same one who brought the Frisian merchants to Haithabu. It was Godfred who halted the conquests of the Frankish Emperor Charlemagne and put an end to the northward expansion of Charlemagne's empire.

By the time Godfred died, in the year 810, the Danes controlled territory as far south as the Eider River on Jutland. Godfred's successor, King Hemming, formalized this fact by a treaty signed in 811. The border of Denmark was to remain on the Eider for more than a thousand years, until a war with Prussia and Austria pushed it north to its present location in 1864.

Although Godfred and Hemming were both kings of all Denmark, their effective power was concentrated in trading centers in the south of Jutland. In the north, conditions were more chaotic.

After the death of King Hemming, in 812, this chaos grew worse. It was not until the tenth century that the kingdom of the Danes began to unite once more under a strong central ruler—Harald Gormsson, who was also known as Bluetooth.

Political life in Norway during pre-Viking and early Viking times was far less orderly than it was in Denmark.

The Norwegians divided themselves into a great many small states that were based on the original clans. Each one of these mini-states had its own assembly—or *thing*—where free clansmen could settle their own disputes and make their own laws. Some of the mini-states were divided into even smaller districts—all of which had their own district *things*.

This of course was democracy in its purest sense. One would have to go all the way back to Athens and the other democratic city-states of ancient Greece to find examples to equal it. However, the Norwegian system had the same flaw as that which helped to destroy the Greek experiment: too many comparatively weak states continually squabbling with one another. The situation almost literally cried out for a "man on horseback"—a unifier or conqueror.

The Norwegians did try to create at least a measure of unity through their *thing* system. By the year 900 they had created a pair of super-*things*—or *lagtings* as they were called—one in the eastern part of the country and one in the west. But this was not only a halfway measure; it came too late. The "man on horseback" was already in the saddle.

The man who did achieve Norwegian unity was Harald Fairhair, the son of Halfdan the Black. Halfdan managed to take over several mini-states in the vicinity of present-day Oslo and, using these states as a base of power, his son decided to conquer all of Norway.

Harald took the independent states one at a time, and added them to his growing kingdom. His enemies did manage finally to unite against him for a climactic battle at Hafrsfjord—an event which probably took place sometime between 882 and 887. But Harald won the battle and continued to take over state after state until he controlled the entire country.

Harald lived until about 943. He had plenty of time, therefore, to impose his rule on the newly united country and to set up a system of tax collection. And the independent-minded Norwegian clansmen had plenty of time to resent this and think longingly of "the good old days," when no one could give them orders or take their money.

The situation was an affront to their Viking pride. And while many Norwegians did learn to adjust to it, others would not. Since they weren't able to defeat Harald on the battlefield, the rebels took the only course open to them. They fled the country.

Where did they go? Different places. A large number took to
their ships and sailed westward to Iceland where political conditions
were much like they were in pre-Harald Norway.

But we have gotten miles ahead of our story. There is one important facet of life in Viking Scandinavia that we have not yet touched
upon: religion.

What sort of gods did these doughty farmers, seamen, and merchants worship? In the beginning, at least, they were non-Christian
gods—a fact that made the Vikings all the more fearsome and horrible to the Christian world.

The chief of the Viking gods was Odin—sometimes known as
Woden. Although Odin was worshiped throughout Scandinavia, the
center of his cult was in Denmark and Sweden. He was usually represented as wearing a cloak and a wide-brimmed hat which con-
cealed the fact that he had only one eye. (He had deliberately
sacrificed his other eye to obtain a drink from the Well of Knowledge.) Though most of us are not aware of it, we still honor Odin
when we call his special day of the week "Wednesday"—or "Woden's Day."

Odin was the god of wisdom, magic, and poetry. He could restore
the dead to life, could see into all the different worlds, and knew the
hidden meanings of magical "runes"—or inscriptions. He was also
the god of war and insane fury, with his very name deriving from
the Norse word for furious. When he rode to battle, he did so on an
eight-footed war-horse. He inspired mortal warriors to fight harder
and promised the bravest of those killed in battle an eternity of eat-
ing, drinking, and fighting in a special paradise, Valhalla.

Thor, the god of thunder, took second place to Odin in power.
He was, however, the most beloved of all the Norse gods. In many
areas—Iceland is one example—he was actually worshiped more
than Odin.

Thor was admired for his great physical strength rather than his
brain power. He was thought of as a mighty red-bearded warrior

who carried a marvelous hammer, *Hjollnir*, which represented the
thunderbolt. Thor was well-disposed towards mankind, and his bluff
and explosive nature was more "human"—in the Viking sense of the
word—than that of the fearsome and overwhelming Odin.

It was, perhaps, just this more human side of his character which
allowed Thor to be thought of as the special patron of farmers and
the god who was chiefly associated with weddings. As late as the
nineteenth century, indeed, rural Scandinavians would hide a hammer—representing the hammer of Thor—in the bed of a newly
married couple.

Like Odin, Thor has given his name to one of our modern days—
Thursday or Thor's Day. So for that matter has the Norse god Tyr,
a now all-but-forgotten deity who lent his name to Tuesday.

At one time, the cult of Tyr was widespread throughout the Teutonic world. He was not only worshiped in the Scandinavian

countries, but—under the name of Tiw—in England as well. Tyr was the god of justice and treaties. He was invoked at the conclusion of a war and was supposed to insure that the terms agreed upon were actually carried out.

These were just a few of the gods that the Norsemen worshiped in pre-Christian days. They even had an entirely separate race of deities called the Vanir who were basically gods of fertility and peace. The most important of the Vanir race were Njorther, a god of sailors and fishermen, and Frey, a harvest and fertility god.

So far, we have not looked at any of the Norse goddesses. They did exist. The most powerful of them were probably Frigg, the wife of Odin (who lent her name to Friday), and Frey's wife, Freyja.

In general, however, the goddesses were not as important as the gods. Norse society was a masculine-oriented one which valued fierceness, honor, and courage in battle above all else. It is little wonder that their goddesses did not have the importance for them that such goddesses as Pallas Athene, Aphrodite, or Hera had for the ancient Greeks.

An eleventh-century statue of Frey, the fertility god.

Like all peoples, the Norse had their religious festivals. And like the festivals of most peoples, theirs fell at midwinter and midsummer.

To us today, the Norse midwinter festival is especially interesting since we have borrowed so many of its trappings—even its name, *Jul* or Yule—and blended them with the festival of Christmas.

The Norse Yule celebrated light, fertility, and rebirth—all of which may seem strange in a festival held in midwinter, on the shortest and darkest day of the year. But we have to keep in mind that once midwinter is reached, the days will grow longer, spring and summer are surely coming, and new life is starting to stir under the earth. The Norse were a people who were far closer to nature than we are. To them, the idea of summer's rebirth in the midst of cold and darkness had an awesome significance.

At Yule, very special honor was paid to the fertility god, Frey, and to the god of farmers, Thor. A boar—the animal sacred to Frey —was used in the festivities, as well as a goat for Thor. The great feast of Yule with its enormous quantities of food and drink is echoed today in our own Yuletide feasts.

Early Scandinavia's midsummer festival honored the end of the sowing of crops and looked forward to harvest time. Midsummer Night—the longest night of the year and, in the northernmost sections of "The Land of the Midnight Sun," a night when darkness never falls at all—was considered to be extremely potent in magic.

Still another important Viking holiday was a mysterious spring festival which was held once every nine years at certain sacred locations such as Uppsala in Sweden and Lejre in Denmark. Little is known about this festival, but it was probably some sort of fertility rite similar to those practiced by other pagan peoples.

III.

Their Marvelous Ships

We do not know precisely what it was that formed the unique Teutonic temperament which differed even from that of other cold-climate peoples. We can't say where their drive came from—their urge to expand and conquer. Though the causes remain a mystery, however, we can pinpoint the technological accomplishment which allowed those later Teutons, the Vikings, to be the great explorers that they turned out to be. It was their mastery of the craft of ship design.

It was not always that way in Scandinavia. In the early days, before the Viking era, the Norsemen were a good distance behind many sections of Europe in both shipbuilding and navigation.

Of course they had boats. Living as they did close to the sea—dependent as they were upon fishing for a large part of their food supply—it is a fair assumption that the Vikings had always built boats of one sort or another. And archaeologists have strengthened this assumption by finding Stone Age fishing implements, such as heavy fishhooks, harpoons, and the like, which were obviously made to be used from boats at sea.

What were these primitive northern boats like? In order to ride the waves and take the stress of offshore waters, they had to be light, strong, and pliant. At the same time, naturally, they had to be watertight. The only primitive class of vessel which fulfills all these requirements is the skin-boat.

This conclusion is backed up by Stone Age rock carvings found in northern Norway. The boats pictured in the carvings appear to be made from the skins of animals stretched over a frame, and from the look of them we can get a fairly good idea of what a typical primitive Norse skin-boat must have been like.

Its bow was higher than its stern and curved up into what was probably an animal head decoration. One of its more interesting features was its hull, which was apparently divided into three sections for greater strength, with the fisherman sitting snugly in the central section. It had no sail and was powered by means of oars or paddles.

Stone Age boats made out of hollowed-out logs have also been found in Scandinavia. But these vessels would have been much clumsier than the skin-boats and could not have ridden the offshore waters nearly as well. In all likelihood they never went to sea at all but were confined to lakes and streams.

Skin-boats continued to be built in the north well after the Stone Age. But, by the early Bronze Age, a new development was also taking place. This was the construction of vessels with hulls made from wooden planks.

The early plank-boats were made from overlapping pine boards which were sewn together with cords of twisted gut. Waterproofing was achieved by caulking between the boards with a substance that contained wool. The hulls were ribbed to give them greater rigidity.

These boats seem to have borrowed their general shape and construction from the earlier skin-boats. The idea of ribbing, for instance, was first used in the skin-boats.

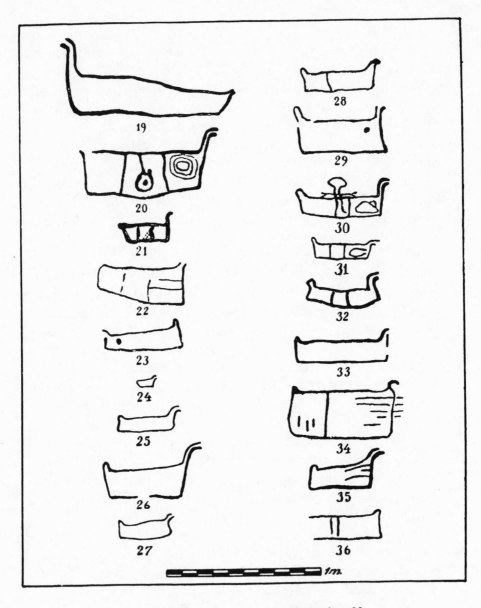

Skin-boats from Stone Age rock carvings in northern Norway.

The log boat.

An eel fork from the Viking period.

All through the Bronze Age and into the early Iron Age, the Scandinavian plank-boats grew in both size and complexity. Later Bronze Age rock carvings picture large, heavy vessels with space provided for many oarsmen. One picture represents a good-sized ship carrying a crew of no less than eighty-one men. The ships' keels curved gracefully and some of them were decorated with animal heads at the bow and stern.

By the end of the Bronze Age, the Norsemen were building boats with keel-boards firmly attached to the skeleton of the hull. The planking was placed over the hull frame and buttressed by the ribs. These boats were hardly as advanced as many of those built in the Mediterranean area, but by no stretch of the imagination could they have been called primitive.

At around this time, however, commerce and trade fell off in all sections of the ancient world. Ships no longer needed to carry such large numbers of men or large amounts of cargo over such long distances. Since the north was no exception to this general rule, the Norse ships were made smaller and more maneuverable. Although they were still built on the basic design which had been developed in earlier times, their planking was lighter and thinner than that of the Bronze Age vessels. Two oars—one at the bow and one at the stern —were used for steering.

Beginning at about A.D. 200, a series of new developments took place which were to lay the foundation for the extraordinary ships of the Viking period.

The first development—seemingly a minor one, but actually of prime importance—was the construction of oarlocks.

At that time and for many years to come, the Norse boats were still solely dependent upon oars for their propulsion. In itself, this was rather a strange thing. Sailing vessels had been used in the Mediterranean since before the start of recorded history. Sails had been used by the ancient Egyptians; they are mentioned in Homer's *Od-*

Rock carvings with ancient Viking inscriptions and pictures give us a good idea of what primitive Norse boats looked like.

yssey and they were an important feature of both the Phoenician galleys and the great merchantmen of the Roman Empire.

Why weren't sails used by the Scandinavians? No one can say. Norsemen had been bred to the sea at least as much as the ancient

Egyptians or Romans. And there was certainly trading contact between the Mediterranean and the north. Yet, among the Scandinavians, the idea of using sails did not take hold.

This is why the oarlock was so important. Before its employment, the Norse literally had to paddle their boats with oars. With this discovery—probably made in Scandinavia—they could actually row them, with the oarlock acting as a fixed fulcrum for the lever action of the oar. This development gave the Norse boats greater speed and control and added greatly to the growing Scandinavian mastery of the sea.

The next two important steps in north-country nautical design had to wait for another four centuries. These steps were the invention of the true keel and the Norse method of steering.

The Norse had used a kind of rudder, naturally, ever since they began to build their larger boats. But this was merely an unfastened

At first, the Norse boats were dependent solely on oars for their propulsion. The development of oarlocks gave them greater speed and maneuverability and added greatly to the growing Scandinavian mastery of the sea.

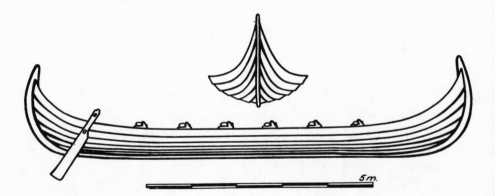

5 m.

oar by means of which a seaman could steer. Usually there was a single steering-oar at the rear of the ship. Sometimes there were two steering-oars, one at the rear and one at the front.

Around the year 600, however, a boat was built with a rudder firmly fixed to the side of its hull towards the rear. The handle of the rudder extended into the boat so that it could be easily controlled from the rearmost seat where the steersman sat.

This was a vast improvement over the loose steering-oar system. It took advantage of the lever plus fixed-fulcrum principle in much the same way that the earlier development of the oarlock had. Now the man at the helm of a Scandinavian vessel could really control it. He could turn it as sharply as he wished without having to worry about an unexpected wave or current wresting the steering-oar overboard.

Just how successful the new system was is shown by the fact that it was used by all the Norse ships of the Viking era. Their rudders were placed near the stern at the side of the ship where they could add to the vessel's stability as well as steer it.

The first boat we know of to have this system was found in Kvalsund, Norway, in 1920. The Kvalsund boat is also notable for having the other improvement which came at about the same time as did the new rudder system: a true keel.

Under the broad keel-board of the Kvalsund boat was an outer runner that served the function of an external keel. To be sure, this was a modest kind of keel. But a keel it was. It strengthened the bottom so that the hull of the vessel could be broader than it was in earlier ships. This in turn permitted a craft of a given length to transport more men and more provisions.

But designing boats with keels did something else as well. It permitted them to carry masts and sails.

Without a keel, a ship's hull would simply split apart under the extra weight of a mast and the extra tension of a windblown sail. Without a fixed rudder, it would be extremely difficult to keep a sailing vessel steady on a true course. With the keel and fixed rudder, however, the Norse were ready to take the next step and design their sailing ships.

For another three hundred years or so, the basic design of the "Kvalsund" hull was improved and strengthened. Vertical cross-sections were built into the keel to give it greater solidity and staying power. The hull was formed of a continuous course of planks and braced by internal cross-beams. This arrangement added to the flexibility of the craft.

The Norse attached a mast and sail to the Kvalsund design by fixing a large block of wood above the keel in the center of the vessel. The mast was fitted into a hollowed-out socket in the wooden block.

These early sailing ships carried a single sail—as indeed would the later Viking vessels. The sails were square in shape and their rigging kept as simple as possible. Rowing was still the most dependable form of power, and the sails could only be employed when the wind was coming from the proper direction.

At the same time that the development of a keel permitted broader hulls, their sides became higher. The oarlocks, therefore, which were set atop the sides of the hulls, forced the blades of the oars into the water at too sharp an angle. To correct this, oar-holes were cut into the vessels' sides.

The end results of these changes and improvements were the first true Viking vessels. It was in ships of this design that the Viking expansion began.

A Viking's ship was his most prized possession. We know this because it was customary to bury with people the things they valued most. A farmer might be buried with his farm tools, his household weapons, even his horse. His wife might be laid to rest with her cooking and sewing utensils. The higher a person's rank, naturally, the more costly and elaborate were the possessions placed in his or her tomb. One Viking queen even had a female slave buried with her.

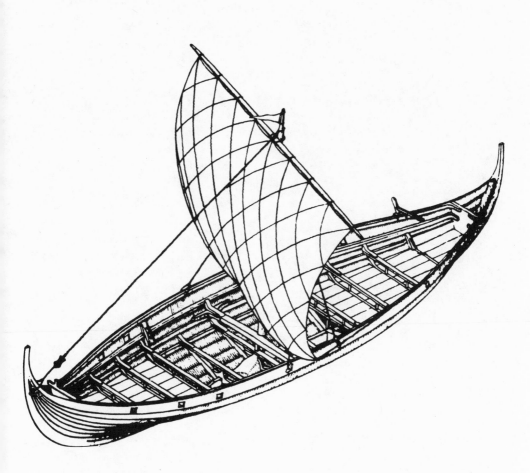

Another development was the use of mast and sail. The sails were square in shape and their rigging kept as simple as possible. This small merchant ship is only forty-four feet long; nevertheless, ships of this type handled most of the trade in the Baltic during the Viking period. The cargo was stored amidships between the half-decks at stem and stern.

Probably the reason was to give the dead person everything he'd need to live in the next world in the same manner as he had lived in this one. It was for this reason that the ancient Egyptians and other pagan peoples practiced similar burial customs.

Some of the most eminent of the early Vikings were buried with

Some Viking chieftains were buried with their most important possessions, their ships. These boat graves are among the largest ever found in Sweden. Together they measure about 325 feet in length and are believed to be something like fifteen hundred years old.

their most important possessions of all: their ships. The best preserved of all the Viking vessels, in fact, have been found in these graves.

Most of the "boat-graves," as they are now known, have been found in Sweden and Norway—although at least one has been located in Denmark. Of all the Viking warships we have, the one in best condition was found in a grave near the Oslo Fjord in Gokstad, Norway. It was uncovered in the year 1880.

The Gokstad ship was an early warship, built well before A.D. 900. Of the basic type we have just finished discussing, it was constructed of oak throughout and was fitted for sixteen pairs of oars, as well as mast and sail.

The ship was clearly designed to make long voyages. No less than three smaller boats were carried in its bow, and it was provided with one state bed plus six lesser beds—all of which could be taken apart when not in use. The ship was an open one, as were all Viking ships. But a tent could be raised over the hull to provide cover when needed. Smaller tents and cooking utensils were carried for the use of landing parties.

How seaworthy was the Gokstad ship? Very. This was proved conclusively in 1893, when an exact replica of it was sailed to America in order to take part in the Chicago World's Fair.

Not far from the Gokstad grave mound was the site of still another important boat-grave, the Oseberg mound, uncovered in 1904. The Viking boat found at Oseberg was in even better condition than the Gokstad ship.

The Oseberg ship was not a war boat. It was a woman's ship— the personal craft of a Viking queen. If the archaeologists are right, the woman with whom the ship was buried was none other than the famous Queen Asa whose grandson, Harald Fairhair, united all of Norway. The ship itself was built during the first part of the ninth century and is at least a generation older than the Gokstad ship.

The Oseberg boat was probably designed as a pleasure craft to be used chiefly in shallow waters. It was made broad of beam and had a shallow draft or underwater depth. It carried a sail, of course, and was powered by fifteen pairs of oars.

The ship was provisioned with everything that Queen Asa, her companions, and her crew might need to live aboard it. Not only did it come equipped with such nautical necessities as an anchor and a gangplank, but it held beds (two of which were large and ornately carved with animal heads), tools, kitchen supplies, and such food-stuffs as flour and fruit. For land transportation, it carried an intricately carved wagon and four sleds. The remains of four dogs, fifteen horses, and an ox were also found on board.

Grave robbers were at the site before the archaeologists came and managed to run off with any items of jewelry that had been buried with the vessel and its royal owner. But many women's goods were

The Oseberg ship. This was a woman's ship—the personal craft of a Viking queen. Built during the first part of the ninth century, it lay in its grave until 1904 when it was uncovered by archaeologists.

One of the ornately carved beds from the Oseberg ship.

left, including sewing equipment and the remnants of clothing and intricate tapestries that were apparently woven by the queen or her ladies.

It should now be clear that, as the Norse entered the Viking Age, they began to specialize their ships. Different ones were made to serve specific functions.

Since it is a woman's ship, many women's things were found buried with the ship, such as sewing equipment, clothing, and tapestries like this one. Jewelry had been stolen by grave robbers before the archaeologists got there.

Although both the Oseberg and the Gokstad ships, for example, were about the same size, and both were open vessels, they were designed to do two different things. The queen's ship from Oseberg was a highly maneuverable pleasure craft. It was not as fast as the Gokstad ship and could not handle long, arduous voyages. As a lady's "yacht," on the other hand, the Gokstad ship would have been clumsy and inefficient.

The most famous class of Viking ship was the "longship"—the ship-of-war. As its name suggests, the longship was long in proportion to its width—a design that made it a fast-moving fighting craft.

Although the longship developed from the Gokstad type of ship, that type itself was not yet a true longship. It was not designed to fight battles at sea, for example, but to transport men who would do their fighting on land. It was later in the Viking period that ships grew larger and heavier in order to improve fighting capacity.

They grew longer, too. The Gokstad ship had thirty-two oars. Within another hundred years or so, forty-oar vessels were the standard size for longships, and many were longer than that. By the year 1000, there were three official categories of Norse longships: the "great ships," with sixty or more oars; the "twenty-thwarters," with forty oars (a "thwart" was the space between the ribs of a ship and there was one pair of oars to each thwart), and the smaller long-ships.

Of course none of these ships—not even the largest—look like what most of us would call a ship at all. They were all open to the elements, with a single line of rowers, and no decks or holds. We might even call them overgrown rowboats with masts stuck in the middle.

But this would be to make a mistake that other nations in the Norse era never made—or at least not twice. The brilliant simplicity of Viking design made their vessels swift, seaworthy, and more than a match in battle for any other ships they were likely to meet.

Some time after the year 870, King Harald Fairhair of Norway built a ship named *Dragon* which he had decorated with a dragon's head at the prow. Apparently, this was the first time that was done. But in the years to follow, the dragon's-head motif grew more and more popular with Scandinavian shipbuilders and was used to decorate ships of all types. It was for this reason that the Viking ships were also known as "dragon ships."

Why the head of a dragon and not some other animal as in their earlier boats? The answer to this may lie in the Norse pagan religion where the dragon or great serpent—the two symbols tended to blend into one another—occupied a position of prime importance. One of the most enduring of all the ancient Teutonic symbols, in-

This painting by Paul Danielson shows a typical Viking warship with its dragon's head at the prow. These decorations, created by King Harald Fairhair of Norway, caused Viking ships to be known as "dragon ships."

deed, is the *Midgardsomr*—an earth-girdling sea serpent that is so huge that it must clamp its teeth around its own tail.

In pagan times, the ships' dragon heads had a specific magical function. They protected the ship and its crew from enemy spirits who wanted to do them harm. That the Vikings took this function seriously is proved by an early Icelandic law ordering all ships to take down their dragon heads when facing the shore lest they frighten the friendly spirits who lived on the land.

After the Norse were converted to Christianity, though, they slowly came to forget the pagan reasons behind these fierce-looking figureheads. The dragon became a decorative symbol of Norse power—somewhat in the fashion that the bald eagle has become symbolic of American power. By the time the final great ships were constructed, it is doubtful that any educated Viking thought of the dragon heads as having magical significance.

They were still used, however. The very last of the great Viking battleships—the *Kristsuden*, launched in 1263—had dragon heads both fore and aft. The two renditions had a bright, gay appearance and were liberally inlaid with gold.

The Viking dragon head was not reserved for warships alone. It was also placed on the prows of the Norse merchant ships to protect commerce.

Although the Norse merchant ships could be used as fighting vessels when necessary, their main duty was to transport cargo. Capacity and staying power were more important than bursts of speed. These ships were wider, rounder, and had a deeper draft than the longships, and could therefore be manned by proportionately fewer crewmen. This design also tended to make them more durable than ships planned primarily for battle.

There were three basic categories of Viking merchant craft: the *byrding*, the *busse*, and the *knarr*. The knarr was the largest of the three and was a true ocean-going vessel. Its rigging was designed to let it sail well into the wind and not merely before it. The knarr handled obediently and needed a crew of only from fifteen to twenty men.

In many respects the knarr was the most remarkable of all the Viking craft—more remarkable even than the more glamorous battleships. It was in their practical knarrs that the Vikings sailed to Iceland, Greenland, and America.

The knarr was given a chance to show its mettle in 1932 when a replica of one of these little ships—it was just sixty feet long—sailed westward on one of the southern routes first pioneered by Christopher Columbus. The knarr cut as much as thirty percent from Columbus's time. Just to prove that this sailing feat was no accident, the Viking replica returned to Norway by way of Newfoundland.

However marvelous the Viking ships were, though, they still had to be guided from point to point. It was not enough for a Viking captain to stumble onto a new territory—a spot on Greenland, for example, or on the North American continent. In order to plant a colony there, the Norse had to be able to find it again. In other words, they had to navigate the ocean.

Nowadays we do that sort of thing as a matter of course. Our own sea captains are well trained in navigation and have a large battery of navigational instruments at their command.

But how did they do it in Viking times? The early Norse did not have the magnetic compass. They did not have our highly accurate charts, although there's little doubt that they did make charts of their own. The sextant—indispensable to us in determining latitude and longitude from the angles of heavenly bodies—was not invented until the eighteenth century. As for a method of finding longitude—that is, a position described in terms of east and west—it was not to be possible for ships at sea until the invention of the ship's chronometer in the year 1714.

But even so, the Norse did navigate.

They did so partly through the use of landmarks.

Replica of an ancient Viking longship, anchored in the harbor of Jossefors, Sweden.

When the Vikings crossed the Atlantic, they took a route which allowed them to spend most of the journey in the coastal waters of Iceland, Greenland, and the smaller North Atlantic islands. When they left one of these points to head into open sea, the steersman could pick out a landmark, steer his ship away from it at the correct angle, and keep looking back at it until the landmark disappeared over the horizon. Then—using the sun, moon, or stars as reference —he could keep his ship on a true course until the next familiar landmark appeared on the horizon ahead of him. This open sea portion of the crossing rarely lasted more than thirty-six hours—about two hundred miles.

And furthermore, even though the Vikings were not able to find their longitude, they were able to locate their latitude—their position in terms of north and south. The sagas have several references to an instrument by which they did this. A description of the instrument is not given, but it was probably similar to the "astrolabe" which the ancient Greeks had used before 150 B.C. The Greek astrolabe was a carved wooden disk with a rotating straight edge. It allowed them to find their latitude at sea by determining the *azimuth*, the position of a star in its regular arc across the sky.

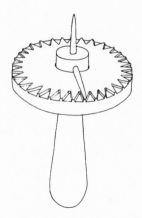

A Viking navigational instrument.

Since the Vikings did not have the magnetic compass, some experts believe that they used a "sun compass," which works on the principle of a reverse sundial. If a Viking mariner knew either his correct latitude or the correct time of day by the sun, the sun compass would have given him his direction.

There is also a theory that the Vikings had a device which permitted them to locate the sun's position even when it was hidden by heavy clouds or fog. This theory is a doubtful one, based on a vague reference in the sagas to certain magical "sun stones" and the fact that there are crystals found in Scandinavia which do have a polarizing effect on light. It is possible that these crystals may be the legendary sun stones.

But even if they are not—even if the Norse had neither magical sun stones nor scientific sun compasses, but were forced to navigate solely through their memory of landmarks and their elementary knowledge of astronomy—the fact is they did navigate. They did sail their knarrs from Norway to Iceland on regular trading voyages. They did travel from Iceland to their colonies on Greenland. And from Greenland they went on to what they called Vinland—what we call America.

But the first step—the first real challenge to the Vikings as North Atlantic navigators—was the trip from Scandinavia to Iceland.

IV.
Iceland

The Vikings were not the first to discover Iceland. That honor apparently belongs to Celts and Picts who sailed there from the northern section of Britain in the fourth century B.C.

When the Greek explorer and geographer Pytheas of Massilia came to Britain in 330 B.C., Celtic and Pictish sailors led him to a large, northern island some six days away by boat. Pytheas called the island Thule and wrote down a fair description of it. From this description, a good many scholars believe that Thule was what we call Iceland—which would make Pytheas, who came from the Mediterranean coast of France, the first nonnorthern European to have reached it.

The Celts and Picts were frequent early visitors to Iceland. They did not found any colonies there, however; at least not for a while. Coins of Roman-British origin have been found in the eastern part of the island, which suggests that there may have been a colony of Celts or Picts there during the Roman era.

It is almost certain, however, that there was a colony of Irish

Celts on Iceland by the seventh or eighth century. Archaeologists digging in Iceland have unearthed Irish artifacts which date from around that period.

There are no written records from that period to back up the archaeological evidence. But there are historical works from medieval times which do lend the theory further support. In his *Book of Iceland*, the early twelfth-century Icelandic historian, Ari Thorgilsson, wrote that Christian people were on that island when the Norsemen got there. When these Christians, whom the Norse called "Papas," moved out of Iceland they left behind certain of their possessions—such as Irish books and bells. These possessions, the historian pointed out, gave proof of their origins. The other famous early work of Icelandic historical scholarship, the *Landnámabók*, meaning *Book of Settlements*, tells much the same story.

Though the medieval historians do not tell us when the Irish first settled on Iceland, they do tell us the Irish left there soon after the Vikings arrived. Ari Thorgilsson stated that this was because the Irish did not wish to live among heathens—meaning, of course, the Vikings themselves.

This has a logical ring to it. Iceland was not converted to Christianity until the year 1000. The Celts from Ireland might well have believed the Norse to be what all Christians thought they were: the "heathen" scourge of Europe—an implacable foe, all but invincible in battle, who must surely be possessed of the devil.

The "Papas" most likely fled in fear of their lives.

The first Viking to visit Iceland was a man with roots in all three Scandinavian nations. His name was Gardar Svavarsson and, while born a Swede, he had married a Norwegian woman and owned some property on the Danish island of Sjælland.

During the 860's Gardar was making a voyage to the Hebrides—a group of islands located off Scotland—when a fierce storm carried his vessel into Icelandic waters. Impressed by the great island, he decided to name it Gardarholm after his own name.

It was shortly after this bid for personal immortality that a Norwegian Viking named Naddod found his own ship storm-tossed into the waters of the same island. Not realizing that Gardar was there ahead of him, Naddod named the place Snowland.

When he and his crew returned to Norway, all Naddod could talk about was "Snowland" and what a marvelous place it was. He was so convincing on the subject that another Norwegian, Floki Vilgerdsson, decided to fit out a ship, load his cattle on it, and leave Norway for good.

"For good" turned out to be a single winter. Floki neglected to bring along enough hay for his cattle and, since they could not find enough fodder there, the beasts all died of starvation. The fishing was fine, Floki admitted when he returned home, but the island was so harsh otherwise that it should be called "Iceland" instead of "Snowland"—and this, according to the Norse, was how Iceland got the name it still has.

But if Floki was embittered by his experience, not everyone on his expedition felt the same way. A young peasant named Thorolf was particularly impressed at what he saw, and took the trouble to say so at every opportunity. Butter actually dripped from the grass, Thorolf reported in one burst of enthusiasm.

The fate of Iceland was still not settled in the winter of 873–74 when a pair of Norwegian foster brothers and cousins got into trouble with the law. The duo, Ingolf Arnarson and Leif Hrodmarsson, had been on a Viking voyage with three young noblemen. Upon their return they quarreled with the noblemen and killed two of the three.

Norse authorities were often tolerant. But murder—especially murder of important young nobles—was something else again. Since Leif had been the cause of the fight, all of his worldly goods and possessions were confiscated in retribution.

Since being down and out in early Norway was not something that any thinking Viking would willingly agree to, Leif decided to leave the country and his cousin Ingolf made up his mind to go with

Statue of Ingolfur Arnarson, the first settler of Iceland, by famous Icelandic sculptor Einar Jonsson.

him. Since they had already visited Iceland briefly and liked what they found there, that island was their destination.

Their first step was to spend the rest of the winter there in order to learn whether Iceland was truly fit for permanent settlement. It was. By the end of the winter they had no doubts left. Iceland was for them.

But there was still the matter of money. The cousins had no ambition to spend the rest of their lives on Iceland as hermits, after all. And to bring their families, slaves, and other necessities to Iceland they needed the wherewithal.

Ingolf, therefore, went back to Norway to sell the property he still had there. But Leif—left destitute because of the murders—had to get his money another way. He went to Ireland on a plundering voyage.

When Leif returned from Ireland with all the loot he needed—including ten Irishmen taken as slaves—the cousins fitted out their ships with cattle, goods, freemen, and slaves and prepared to set sail.

From the very beginning, Ingolf and Leif went about things differently. Leif, who had apparently become partly Christianized in Ireland, refused to sacrifice to Odin, Thor, and the other Teutonic gods. Nor would he permit his dwelling-place on Iceland to be determined in the traditional Viking way: by tossing the "wooden pillars of his high seat" into the ocean in order to see where the waves cast them ashore. (These "pillars," incidentally, were actually the front legs of a Viking lord's official chair. They were made extremely tall to continue up past the seat of the chair and touch the roof of his house. When the Viking changed his residence, he would take the "pillars" with him.)

According to the pious pagans of the day, it was because Leif refused to follow the tradition of casting his seat pillars into the ocean that his eventual fate was so sad. During his first spring on Iceland, he and the other male Vikings in his party were killed by his Irish slaves, while the women were taken as captives. The possibility that the Irishmen might have harbored some justifiable resentment against Leif for taking them as slaves in the first place was naturally not dwelt upon by the Norse commentators.

Ingolf, on the other hand, behaved like a proper Viking. He made all the correct sacrifices to the gods and threw the pillars of his high seat into the sea as soon as his ship reached Iceland. The pillars disappeared into the waters and Ingolf and his people went to see where they landed.

Ingolf was still searching for his pillars when he came across the bodies of Leif and his men. After reflecting upon the sad fate of all those who do not perform the Viking rituals, Ingolf buried the Norsemen and went off to avenge the deed. He caught up with the

Irishmen on a nearby island, killed them, and took the women under his own protection.

Ingolf did not find his seat pillars until the spring of 875. When they were finally located it was at a spot halfway around the island —a coastal region which abounded in natural hot springs. Ingolf called the place Smoky Creek—or, in Norse, *Reykjavik*—and settled down there. Reykjavik is still the name of the capital of Iceland. It stands on the spot where Ingolf Arnarson's high seat pillars were finally washed ashore.

Ingolf and his cousin were the first real Norse settlers on Iceland. But a whole flood of Norsemen followed them there. The next sixty years became known as the period of "settling the land"—the *land-náma* period. At its end—during the 930's, that is—Iceland could boast a population of not less than twenty thousand people.

The chief reason for this enormous rush to Iceland was to be found back in Norway: King Harald Fairhair.

We have already seen how Harald gained control of that country by conquering one small independent state after the other until he could proclaim himself ruler of the entire land. And we have also seen that a good many of his Viking subjects—whose feelings about their own personal freedom ran deep indeed—decided that they could not live happily under the new setup.

What we do not know is how those who made up their minds to stay on in Norway felt about all this. Were they delighted to be rid of a bunch of troublemakers? Was Norway itself a far more pleasant place after they departed? Or was Harald's Norway a brutish dictatorship that anyone would flee if only he had the means?

There is no way of knowing. All we can do is remember that there are at least two sides to every story. And while some of Harald's actions were certainly barbaric, many of those who fled his rule were—like Leif Hrodmarsson, for example—among the least upstanding members of their communities.

As for Harald himself, he was less than delighted at the departure of so many members of his aristocracy. No matter how troublesome they were or how difficult to control, they still paid large sums of money in the form of taxes to the royal treasury.

Harald tried to correct this loss of revenue in a couple of ways. First of all, he imposed a departure tax upon all of his subjects who moved out of Norway. Secondly, he claimed sovereignty over Iceland.

Although there were always evaders, the king was at least partially successful in collecting his departure tax. But his second idea was an utter failure. As long as Iceland didn't want him to rule it, he couldn't. It was too far away to be controlled by force.

At one point, Harald sent a man, Uni, to the island with orders to bring it under royal control, promising him a large reward if he succeeded. At first glance, Uni might be considered a good choice for the mission. His father was Gardar Svavarsson, the Swedish-born Viking who was the first Scandinavian to set foot on Iceland. But this family background did not influence the Icelanders. Uni was largely ignored by the settlers and went home again having accomplished nothing.

Many of those who were among the first settlers came to Iceland from Viking colonies outside of Scandinavia.

By the landnáma period, there were a good many of these colonies in the British Isles. There were colonies in Scotland, for example, as well as in Ireland, the Shetland Islands, the Orkneys, the Hebrides, and other places. Some of the Vikings in the British colonies had come there from Norway in order to escape Harald's new laws without having to make the crossing all the way to Iceland.

But Harald Fairhair had a long arm. And the nearer colonies were well within its reach. He proved this over and over again. In the 920's, for example, when Norse exiles in Scotland and the other settlements began to make increasingly daring raids against the west coast of Norway, Harald set out systematically to punish them.

He organized a large fleet and headed first for the western coast of Scotland. After dealing with the Viking settlements there, he sailed to the Hebrides, the Orkneys, and the Shetland Islands. Everywhere he went he removed rebellious Norse chiefs—putting to death as many of them as he could—and replaced them with his own men.

Those rebels who managed to survive Harald's purges did not have many alternatives. A few tried hiding in the outer islands. Others joined the exodus to Iceland.

But everyone who came to Iceland during the landnáma period did not do so because they disliked King Harald. One early settler, for instance, Ragnvald Möre-jarl, was a close friend of the Norwegian king. Still another, Ingimund the Old, fought at Harald's side in the important battle of Hafrsfjord.

Why did men such as these—and there was a good number of them—join with those who were feuding with the king in order to live and work in Iceland? The basic answer has to lie in the island's vast areas of new land. The Norsemen, like the American pioneers who crossed the continental divide in covered wagons, were bent on making their fortunes in what was still open territory.

In the beginning, at least, the territory was truly open. Any settler could have as much land as he was able to work. Having his choice, he probably selected property on the south and west coasts of the island, which were washed by the warm and gentle waters of the Gulf Stream. As more and more settlers poured in, however, all the best land was taken up and quarrels broke out over what was left.

King Harald Fairhair, who was still trying to rule Iceland from his throne in Norway, set down an edict to deal with the land problem. No one, the new law stated, would be permitted to take more property than he and his ship's crew could walk around in a single day.

The edict was probably a reasonable one. But its enforcement by Harald was another matter. Chances are that it—like most of Harald's Icelandic pronouncements—was simply ignored.

Whatever the fate of the land-holding law, new settlers continued to come to the island. Many of their names—which were recorded and inscribed in the old Icelandic history books as well as in those compilations of fact and fiction known as the sagas—are as well known today in their own country as the early heroes of the American colonies are here. One of the most famous of all was a magnificent Viking lady who was known as Aud the Deep-Minded.

Aud was the daughter of Ketil Flatneb who, in the years between 840 and 860, had been one of the most successful of the Viking raiders. In his old age, however, he had a quarrel with Harald Fairhair and was forced to hide in the Hebrides for fear of his life.

Aud, in the meantime, had married Olaf the White, a Viking raider who had captured Dublin and made himself king of Ireland. When Olaf died in a battle, Aud took their son, Thorstein, to the Hebrides where the lad married and eventually became a king in his own right.

Like his father, Thorstein was killed while fighting. With Harald unrelenting in his feud with Ketil's descendants, and without a son to defend her, Aud realized that she would have to flee the Hebrides with her three granddaughters. She had a ship built secretly and sailed with her freemen, slaves, and household goods to the Orkney Islands.

The matriarch found a husband for one of her granddaughters in the Orkneys. She sailed from there to the Faroes where she found a husband for her second granddaughter. With her father in trouble with the king, however, and many members of her family exiled to Iceland, Aud decided to find a permanent refuge there.

There are many stories told about Aud the Deep-Minded and her great strength of character. One of these tells of her death after the wedding of her youngest granddaughter.

On the wedding night, Aud made a formal gift of her house on Iceland to her new grandson-in-law. She instructed the guests to enjoy themselves and retired to bed. There she died peacefully in her sleep. Looking at her calm face the next morning, the Vikings all marveled at how Aud the Deep-Minded had kept her dignity to the very end.

Another well-known early Icelandic settler was a man named Thorolf Mostrarskegg. Back in Norway, Thorolf had harbored a fugitive brother of Aud's, Björn the Easterner. Furious at this, King Harald sentenced Thorolf to exile.

One more man who came to Iceland during the landnáma period was Skallagrim. Skallagrim is best known as the father of the poet, Egil, who as a boy killed his father's overseer in a fit of rage and as a man wrote a lovely memorial ode about his own son.

The *Landnámabók* contains many other names of Norse pioneers. I have merely mentioned these in order to give you some idea of the great variety of people who were attracted to Iceland during those early days.

As Iceland grew in population, its need for effective government also grew.

According to Harald Fairhair, of course, Iceland already had a government. He ruled the island from Norway. But Harald's authority existed mainly in his own mind. He was never able to control Iceland. And if there were any Icelanders who wanted him to take over, they were extremely few in number.

How then was Iceland governed? The Viking landowners were among the most independent-minded men the world has ever seen. Each one of them controlled his own estate. In the very beginning, at least, they felt that was government enough.

But that situation could not go on forever—even if the Vikings wished that it could. In pre-Harald Norway itself, after all, there had at least been local government, the *thing*. So in Iceland, too, loose associations of neighboring estates got together to form local communities.

These communities, known as *Godords*, were of a semireligious nature. The leader of a Godord was the *Godi*, the priest of the local temple. The Godi was invariably the richest and most powerful Viking in the neighborhood. And since it was his money which built the temple, he simply assumed the largely ceremonial office of priest. He also presided over the thing—the local assembly which the Icelanders had imported from Norway.

This too was a less than satisfactory arrangement, however, with all the built-in problems that the old Norwegian system had. To those Vikings who had lived through the coming of Harald, its weaknesses must have been all too apparent. If they were to save the individual liberty they prized, they had to find a better system of government.

The *Godar* (plural of Godi) came to the same conclusion. They decided to send one of their number, a man named Ulfljot, to Norway in order to study the legal system there. Perhaps it might be adaptable to conditions in Iceland. At the same time, Ulfljot's foster brother, Grim Geitskor, was asked to choose a suitable place for a general assembly on the island.

Ulfljot stayed in Norway for three years. He spent the time well. When he returned to Iceland, he not only brought a suggested code of laws, but an outline for an island-wide constitution.

Ulfljot's recommendations included plans for a national assembly —the *Althing*—which would meet every year for two weeks in the summer. Although parliament was to be attended by every free man on the island, its powers were to be exercised through an inner council consisting of forty-eight godar and ninety-six others.

The first Althing met in the year 930 at *Thingvellir*—the beautiful "Plain of the Thing," which Grim Geitskor had selected as the most fitting spot for such an assembly. Ulfljot's proposals were accepted at that meeting, forming Iceland's constitution and legal system.

The new government was far from a perfect democracy. By its very nature it favored the great landowners who wrote the laws and could bend them to their own purposes. On the other hand, however, it was not only an improvement on the nongovernment Iceland had before, it was a large step in the direction of a representative government.

One more question remains, however. What of Iceland's relationship with Norway? Was the island an independent nation now? A mere colony? Or what?

The answer appears to be a little bit of both. The Vikings themselves had mixed feelings on the subject. While they certainly wanted to be independent, they also felt that they should be in some sort of association with Norway.

As Vikings, they naturally resolved their problem in the most practical way possible. Though Harald Fairhair and his successors were not permitted to interfere in island affairs, the Icelanders decided that the Norwegian throne should have some influence—not authority, but influence—in Iceland.

This allowed the Icelanders to retain their Norwegian citizenship. A dual citizenship, after all, would lend far more trade and economic opportunities to a Viking than would citizenship in Iceland alone.

From the Icelanders' point of view, that would have been the best of all possible deals. The arrangement lasted until King Haakon IV of Norway occupied the island in the thirteenth century and forced the inhabitants to submit to his rule.

At the end of the fourteenth century, Iceland—along with Norway—came under Danish authority. It was not until our own century—in the year 1944—that Iceland became a completly independent and sovereign nation.

But all that is far ahead of the landnáma period of the early settlers and explorers of Iceland and their more immediate descendants. For it was those descendants who—outdoing even their spectacular forebears—left the by then familiar shores of Iceland to explore Greenland and America.

V.

Greenland

———

Eric Thorvaldsson was not one of those Vikings who could be called native Icelanders. He was born and spent his childhood in the Jaeder district of Norway, and remained there with his family until he was fourteen years old. He brought much glory to Iceland, however. And, more than any other person, he was responsible for the westward movement from that island, which led eventually to the Norse discovery of America.

Eric—who is much better known by the descriptive nickname of Eric the Red—was far from a modest, storybook hero. He was a rough pagan with a shrewd mind and a violent temper. He might well have felt at home among the early Goths or Vandals.

Apparently his character resembled that of his father, Thorvald. The sagas—which are often vague about such matters—tell us that Thorvald and Eric had to leave their home in Jaeder because of some murders. Just who was murdered, or why, we do not know.

In any event, Thorvald left Norway for Iceland, taking his wife, his daughter, and his redheaded son with him. The family found land in the relatively barren northwestern section of the island, and settled down to an uneventful life until Thorvald died. Shortly after that, Eric married a girl named Thjodhild and moved south to Haukadal where the country was generally more fertile.

Eric was not on his new farm for very long, however, when he found himself in the middle of a full-fledged feud. The trouble began when a group of his slaves started a landslide which killed a neighboring farmer. Since Eric and his neighbor were not on the friendliest of terms, relatives of the slain man accused Eric of ordering his slaves to do the deed.

This accusation may or may not have been true. The Norse played rough in those days, and Eric was among the roughest. The problem was that at least one kinsman of the dead farmer—a man who is known to us as Eyjolf the Sour—was not satisfied with mere accusations. He had to take action. The action he took was to kill the offending slaves.

It turned out to be an expensive move. Eric retaliated by killing both Eyjolf and a companion.

But if Eric thought that he had now won the argument and would no longer be bothered, he was doomed to disappointment. Killing slaves was one thing, in Viking times, and killing farmers and landowners quite another. Nor could it have helped Eric's cause that he was a Norwegian-born man who was a comparative stranger to Haukadal.

Eric was ordered to appear before the local thing in order to defend himself against the charge of manslaughter. He knew—he must have known—that even if he managed to clear himself somehow, he would still have to face hordes of furious kinsmen bent on revenge. So he took the only course still open to him; he fled.

Eric was in such a rush about leaving, in fact, that he could not even take along the pillars of his high seat. He deposited them with a neighbor, Thorgest, and took his family first to the shores of the Breidenfjord and then to an island in the fjord—the island of Oxney.

Everything went well until Eric paid a secret visit to Thorgest to ask for his seat pillars back, for Thorgest decided that they now belonged to him. Eric took back the pillars anyway and, in the battle which followed, killed two of Thorgest's sons.

By now, Eric had at least these two feuds going. And he was at a decided disadvantage in both. Thorgest was extremely influential, while Eric had a bad reputation as a man of violence. When Thorgest brought legal action against him, he was forced to appear before the thing.

Eric was banished from Iceland for a period of three years. This banishment, which came in the year 981, was the turning point in Eric's life.

As soon as the sentence was pronounced, Eric the Red was a man at bay. For so long as he remained on Iceland, he was fair game for Thorgest and his men. He had to leave the island, and he had no time to dally about it.

He did have a ship, of course. And he had some friends to help him hide from Thorgest while he prepared the ship for sea. He had already determined to sail west.

Why west? What was he looking for there?

According to the sagas, Eric was searching for a then mysterious land first seen by another Viking—Gunnbjorn, son of Ulf the Crow—more than a century before Eric's banishment.

Gunnbjorn had been swept so far westward by a storm at sea that he caught sight of a land as yet unknown. Eric wanted to find out for himself if the story was true—if the islands and mainland which Gunnbjorn claimed to have visited really existed.

When Eric set out on his voyage of discovery he soon learned that Gunnbjorn had not lied. He came to the eastern coast of "Gunnbjorn Land" with its great fields of glaciers and sailed down to the southern tip—to that promontory which is now called Cape Farewell. Rounding the cape, he headed his knarr northeast to explore the fjords on the southwest coast of this largest island in the world.

What he found there must have pleased him. The land in this section is the best farming land that Greenland has to offer—something which Eric, a farmer and a son of a farmer, could not have failed to recognize.

The coming of fall interrupted these explorations. Eric and his men had to prepare for the long, dark winter. They spent the cold-weather months on Ericsey, a small island near the entrance of Ericsfjord which is not far from the modern village of Julianhaab.

Once the days grew warmer again, Eric resumed his self-imposed task of investigating the western coast of Greenland. He and his men decided to spend their second winter there on another offshore island, Ericsholm, which is located west of Ericsey, near the place we call Cape Desolation.

Eric had now come to his third summer on Greenland. He did not waste this one either, but sailed north until he had a good idea of the portion of Greenland's western coast best for farming. Then he turned the prow of his knarr south again and returned to Ericsfjord.

Now Eric began a closer inspection of the fjord, sailing inland all the way to its head. It was there, at the head of the northern arm, that he was eventually to build his Greenland home. That project was for the future, however. Now he headed back to Ericsey and prepared to spend the fast-approaching winter there.

The next summer—the summer of 984—saw the end of Eric's period of exile. He was free to return to Iceland.

It would be nice to say that Eric returned to a hero's welcome. He had accomplished, after all, everything he said he would. He'd kept his promise to find the land that Gunnbjorn had seen. And he'd lived to come home to talk about it.

To Eric's old enemy, Thorgest, however—and probably to many others on Iceland as well—he was hardly a hero. To Thorgest, he was still the same old Eric the Red with whom he was feuding. And Vikings being Vikings, it was only natural for Thorgest and his friends to do their best to make Eric feel unwelcome.

But as we've already seen, Eric also had friends on Iceland. When he returned, he stayed with one of them on the offshore island of

Viking feuds were common. This battle is being reenacted by modern-day Scandinavians on one of the many Viking festivals held each year. Eric the Red had to leave Iceland for a period of three years as punishment for manslaughter during a feud. In those three years he made the first explorations of Greenland, another step in the series that led to the Viking journeys to America.

Holmatr. He lived there safely through the winter, but the following spring the running battle with Thorgest began again. They fought a decisive engagement then, and Eric lost.

Strangely enough, the long-term results of this defeat actually worked to Eric's advantage. The loss in battle apparently convinced him that it was time to mend some fences among the Icelanders. Shortly afterwards, he and Thorgest were reconciled. We don't know just how peace was arranged between these two sworn enemies. But since it was Eric who was losing the fight, the major efforts at peacemaking must have come from his side.

This is the first hint of an aspect of Eric which we have not seen before. We have seen him as a brawler, an adventurer, a successful seaman and explorer. Now we can also recognize that he must have been at least enough of a diplomat and salesman to convince a winning enemy to call off a feud.

As it turned out, it was a good thing that he did have some talent in selling, for he was about to launch a scheme in which he'd need all the salesmanship he could muster. The scheme was nothing less than the colonization of Greenland.

But why should Eric want to go anywhere now? He was not about to be banished again. His major feud was ended and his friends had already proved themselves cooperative. There was nothing to prevent him from settling down as a solid Icelandic farmer and citizen.

Nothing except his own nature, perhaps. One cannot help suspecting that it was not enough for Eric to be just another Norseman living however good a life on Iceland. He would prefer to be a leader, even in a rugged, hostile country. He was determined to found his settlement. This meant that he would have to convince people to give up their homes in Iceland and take their chances with him. It would be no easy task to do this. How would he go about it?

His first step was to change the name of the place from "Gunnbjorn's Land" to Greenland.

Why Greenland? If he didn't like the name of Gunnbjorn's Land, he might well have renamed it after himself. He did have every excuse to do so. Gunnbjorn had merely skirted the island—Eric had actively explored it for three years. Nor was he afflicted with an un-Viking sense of modesty—as his habit of naming fjords, islands, and other geographical locations after himself shows.

The reason he named it Greenland, according to the "Saga of Eric the Red," is that "men would be the more readily persuaded to come there if the land had a good name."

And there it is. Eric the adventurer had—temporarily at least—become Eric the Norse advertising man. He wanted to attract settlers and thought that he could do the job better if his prospects could visualize a land where the grass was green and the fields were fertile. It is the same reason that our own real-estate ads describe a new community as "Spring Valley" rather than "Barren Waste" or even "Ericsville."

Eric's scheme worked; he got his settlers. In the summer of 985, a total of twenty-five knarrs left Iceland to carry emigrants and their families across the sea to Greenland.

The crossing was not without its dangers. According to the *Landnámabók*, only fourteen of the ships actually reached their destination. Some of the others were driven back to Iceland once more, while the rest of the ships were lost at sea.

Large merchant ships like the one shown here, with high sides, built of timber, carried settlers and livestock across the Atlantic to Iceland and Greenland and, possibly, even to America. Long voyages in an open boat of this kind must have been bleak, and no doubt a considerable number of these ships went down.

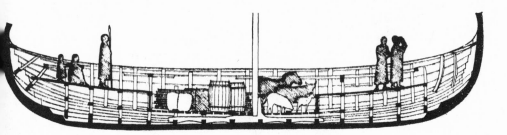

We can only guess at the catastrophe which overtook the expedition. A storm at sea, perhaps. But it could have been no ordinary storm, as Viking ships often made crossings as long as the two hundred miles of open water that separated Greenland and Iceland in all kinds of weather.

Most of the settlers who came to Greenland joined Eric in claiming land in the area of the Ericsfjord. Eric himself had a large holding at the head of its northern arm. He called his estate Brattahlid. And there, during the 1920's, archaeologists from Scandinavia uncovered a one-room building which may have been Eric the Red's house.

It was a long and narrow structure, measuring fifty feet by just over fourteen. There is nothing to indicate what the roof was made of, but the walls were of sod. They were heavy enough to withstand the coldest Greenland winter, however, for in some places they measured as much as twelve feet thick. One of the more elegant features of the house was that it had its own supply of running water. Water from an adjoining spring was carried through a stone pipe to a basin in the center of the floor. One more house—perhaps the home of one of Eric's neighbors—was found near Brattahlid.

The sprawling community near the Ericsfjord became known as the Eastern Settlement. It never had many homesteads—two hundred or so in the period of its greatest growth—but these were spread over such a vast area of land that twelve churches and two monasteries were built to service them during Christian times.

Not all the Greenlanders lived in the Eastern Settlement. Starting in 996, another community was settled about a hundred and seventy miles north of the Ericsfjord. This was the Western Settlement. It consisted of ninety homes and four churches.

As far as is known, these were the only settlements on Greenland during the Viking era. And at the height of the island's rather dubious prosperity, the total populations of both communities were not more than two or three thousand each.

During the summer months the Vikings ranged far north of these

Ruins of a Norse farm during excavations at the Eastern Settlement. Most of the farm buildings here are assembled in one large block: hall and fire-room, sleeping-room and bathhouse, cow-byre and barn. In a storeroom the bottoms of three enormous tubs were found, one of them containing the remains of about a hundred small mice, apparently trapped when searching for food after the farm was deserted sometime during the fifteenth century.

The settlements in Viking Greenland and main sailing routes from them.

homesites in order to hunt such game as whales, seals, and walrus. To aid them in this activity, they constructed summer hunting cabins in the area of Disco Island.

Norse artifacts were actually found farther north than this. A small "rune stone"—that is a stone bearing old Norse writing—was found at latitude 72° 55′. To understand just how far into the Arctic region this is, one only has to remember that the North Cape—the northernmost piece of land on the European continent—is at latitude 71° 07′.

A cairn on the summit of Kingigtorssuaq hid the northernmost trace of the Norsemen. It was here, at latitude 72° 55′, that a small runic stone was discovered in 1824.

Even as Greenland was being settled, an important change was taking place throughout the entire Viking world. The religion of Christianity was coming to supplant the old Teutonic faith.

Norway became officially Christian in 995, and Iceland in the year 1000. The word "officially" is important, because accepting any particular date for something which takes place as gradually as a change in religion is apt to be misleading. Of course there were Christians in the Norse lands for many years before these dates. And of course the old pagan religion was practiced by many for some time after.

Official dates for a change in religion tell us when the ruling body of a nation gives its sanction to the new religion. The year 995 marks the coming to power in Norway of the Christian king Olaf Tryggvesson. And the year 1000 is the year when the Icelandic *Althing* finally agreed to accept Christianity as the state religion of that island.

In that same year—A.D. 1000—Christianity was first introduced into Greenland by Eric the Red's son, Leif, who had been converted to the new faith while he was in Norway.

Leif's mother, Thjodhild, asked to be baptized not long after her son began his missionary work. But Eric himself refused to have anything to do with Christianity. No matter how his wife and son argued and pleaded, he remained steadfastly loyal to Odin, Thor, and the other pagan gods until he died. Thjodhild eventually gave up the obviously useless struggle and, abandoning her husband to his pagan fate, divorced him.

There are no records to show the year Greenland became officially Christian. The fact that Eric was permitted to remain a pagan does not necessarily mean that Christianity was not the state religion during his lifetime. Iceland permitted paganism to be practiced in private until 1016. The Greenland Althing, however, probably voted to accept Christianity within a short time after Iceland's Althing did.

By the middle of the eleventh century, at any rate, Greenland was recognized as a part of the Archbishopric of Bremen. And, in the year 1124, the Greenlanders were considered both important and devout enough to have a bishop of their own appointed by the Church.

By now we have reached the high point of the history of Viking Greenland. The rest of the story is a sad one. And its ending is even sadder.

In the early years Greenland was a politically free state governed by its own Althing which was undoubtedly modeled on the Icelandic Althing. Much of what we said about that older parliament, therefore, we can apply to the Greenland version. Even in the beginning, though, Greenland was more economically dependent on Norway than was Iceland. While both islands depended on Scandinavia as a market for their goods and a supplier of their needs, Iceland—with its greater population and larger area of arable land—could be somewhat more self-sufficient.

The Greenlanders did their best to support themselves by farming, hunting, and fishing. Nevertheless they needed to import not only manufactured items from Europe, but often even such basic necessities as grain and timber. When passing time made Norway gradually indifferent to the welfare of Greenland, the always precarious life of the Greenlanders became even more uncertain.

Adding to this uncertainty, in the thirteenth century, were new troubles closer to home. Starting at that time, the Thule Eskimos began to move into the areas which the Vikings had settled. The Thules originated with a prehistoric Eskimo civilization which apparently had developed in Alaska and gradually spread eastward. Although it took its name from Thule in Greenland, no representatives of that or any other Eskimo civilization were on the island when the Norsemen came. The Vikings fought several engagements with their new neighbors, but just how much conflict there was between the two cultures, and how much this contributed to the decline of the colony, is not known.

During the thirteenth century, the Greenlanders made a desperate bid for European help. They offered to give up their most treasured possession—their independence—for security. The island agreed to become a Norwegian crown colony and pay taxes to the king. In return, all it could have hoped for was more extensive trade with the mother country. In the year 1261, Norway—which was then in the process of taking over the richer, more valuable (and far more unwilling) island of Iceland—accepted the Greenlanders' offer.

But even this failed to stem the decline. The hoped-for boom in trade never took place. The great days of Viking sea power in Europe were nearing their end. Scandinavian merchantmen were being replaced as lords of the sea-lanes by German traders from the Hanseatic League of north German towns, including Hamburg, Bremen, Lübeck, and Danzig.

Indeed, the agreement with Norway made life worse in Greenland, for the Norwegian rulers decided not to permit any more private trade with their colony. Only royal merchantmen, operating out of the port of Bergen, were now permitted to visit Greenland. And fewer and fewer of them did.

By the middle of the fourteenth century, poverty on the island had become so extreme that the Church officially excused Greenland from paying any further tithes. Still conditions grew worse. By the fifteenth century, the descendants of the great Viking explorers were barely managing to stay alive on a diet of dried fish and milk. They were shrinking in stature, too. According to scientists who have studied the skeletons in a fifteenth-century Greenland burial ground, the average height of a man in that period was under five feet. There was not a single woman who measured more than four feet, nine inches when she was alive.

But perhaps even worse than their physical suffering was the demoralization of this once proud people. They had literally forgotten much of what they were. By 1492—when Columbus was making his first voyage to the West Indies—most of the Norse on Green-

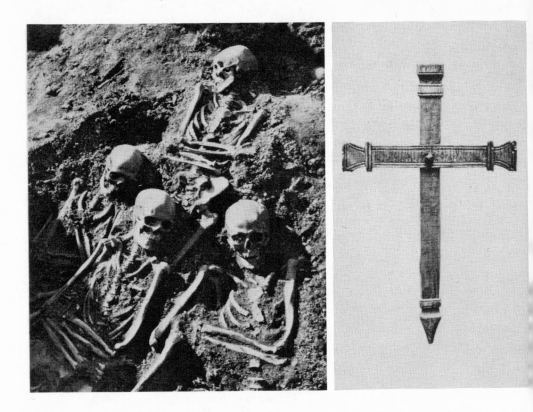

A fourteenth-century description of Greenland mentions about sixteen parish churches in the Norse settlements. Ruins of some of these churches have been found, including one built about the year 1001 at Brattahlid and described in "Eric the Red's Saga." Found in the excavated graves at these sites were well-preserved skeletons and various goods deposited with the dead, including the wooden cross.

land had adopted the culture of the Eskimos. According to a papal letter of that year, the only token they had to remind them of the Christian religion was an altar cloth which was ritually exhibited once each year.

Ships no longer went to Greenland, now. The island was all but forgotten.

Then, in the year 1550, a German ship was blown there by a storm. On board was an Icelander who was surprised to find ruined houses on Greenland which had a familiar Norse appearance. Among the ruins was the body of a man who was dressed in coarse but well-made clothing. By the dead man's side was an old, well-worn knife.

Who was this dead man? It is only a guess, of course, but perhaps he was the last—the very last—of the Greenland Vikings.

Hvalsey Church at the Eastern Settlement, the best-preserved Norse ruin. After a wedding in this church in 1408, the last recorded event in the Greenland settlements, silence and darkness descended.

VI.
The Case for theVikings

On October 12, 1965, newspapers all over America ran stories about a recently discovered map which dated back to the second quarter of the fifteenth century. The owner of the map was one of the nation's most prestigious institutions of higher learning, Yale University. And, according to the experts at Yale, the map—which not only portrayed Iceland and Greenland, but also showed a body of land called "Vinland" possibly representing a portion of North America—was final proof that the Vikings did land on this continent nearly five hundred years before Columbus.

The ink was hardly dry on these stories, however, before a storm of controversy arose. Critics were quickly found to call the "Vinland Map," as it soon became known, a fraud. And even if the map was not a hoax, some of the more vocal of the critics stated, it didn't prove anything, anyway.

Much of this furor was probably caused by emotion. Yale University, for a reason known only to its publicity department, released the story to the press on Columbus Day. Partisans of Christopher

Columbus were quick to take offense. They felt that it was a deliberate attempt to besmirch the reputation of the great Genoese navigator who was the "real" discoverer of America.

Ethnic pride became involved. Italian-American societies tried to outdo each other in denouncing the map, while anyone connected with Scandinavia defended it with equal vigor. Yale's scholars, in the meantime—relying on their own expertise—steadfastly insisted that they had checked it out and found it to be genuine.

Here a question arises: Could the map be a fraud—even in the face of such scholarly assurances to the contrary?

Yes, it could be. Experts have been known to be wrong. They have even been the victims of hoaxes. And if any scholarly expert should ever try to deny this to you, just whisper the magic words, "Piltdown Man," to him and watch his face turn red.

In the year 1912, anthropology experts agreed that a skull found on Piltdown Commons near the town of Lewes in southern England came from a prehistoric man who was an example of the fabled missing evolutionary link between man and ape. They stuck to this agreement for quite some time, and it wasn't until the 1950's that the world learned the truth: The Piltdown skull was actually a forgery made by combining the jaw of an ape with the cranium of a man.

How can we be sure, then, that the Vinland Map is not another scientific hoax which fooled the experts? Of course we can't be sure. But we don't know that it is a hoax, either. And the experts aren't fooled that often. If scientific hoaxes were everyday events, they would hardly be news when they did occur.

There is no way to be absolutely sure that the map is genuine. In order to do that, we'd almost need a time machine which would allow us to peer over the map-maker's shoulder while he worked.

(Overleaf) The Vinland Map, which caused great controversy when its discovery was announced on Columbus Day, 1965.

Volucꝛe dei ꝑꝛ ſẽ i eꝛ liij age ad ſẽ e ſ ꝑꝛceſẽ ẽ i ſẽꝛᵒ ẽ ẽ iꝰ
eſmꝛad cõmẽ ꝗ ꝑᵒꝛeſꝯ ꝑꝛ ẽ ẽ ẽ ꝰ ẽ ẽ ẽ ꝰ ẽꝛi ẽꝛi ꝯ
ẽ eꝛ glaciᵒ ẽ ẽ ꝛ ẽ ẽ li ꝗ ẽ ꝗ ꝗ ẽ ẽꝛi ꝯ ẽ eꝛ ẽ ꝯ ẽ e
Volucꝛe huᷓ ẽ ẽ iẽꝯ ꝗ ꝗ ꝛe ẽ ẽ ꝯ ꝯ ẽꝛaliᵒ humaᷓ
Groẽlãde ꝯꝯꝯ ꝑeꝛ ꝯ ẽ ẽꝛ ꝯ ẽ ẽ ẽꝛ li ẽꝛiᵉ ꝯ ẽ ẽꝛꝯꝯꝯ
ꝗ ꝗ ꝯ eꝛ ꝗ ꝯ ẽꝛ ꝯ ꝯ ẽ ꝗ ꝯꝯ eꝗ ẽ ẽ ꝯ ꝗ ꝯ ꝗ ẽ eꝛ ꝯ ẽ
iꝯꝯꝯ ꝗ ẽꝛ ẽ ẽꝛ ꝗ ꝗ ꝯ ꝯ ẽ ꝯ ꝯ et ẽ ẽꝛẽ ꝑeꝛꝯ ꝯꝯꝯꝯ
ꝯꝯ ẽ eꝛ ẽꝛ eꝗ ꝯ ẽ ꝯ ẽ ẽꝛꝯ ẽ ẽ ꝯ ꝯ ꝑꝛꝯ eꝛ ꝯꝯ
ꝯ ẽ eꝛ ꝯ ꝯ ꝯꝯꝯ ꝯ ꝯ ẽ
ꝯ eꝛ ꝑeꝛꝯ ẽꝯ

Groẽlãdia

Vinlãda Inſula
à Byarno repᵃ
et leiphᵒ ſocⁱⁱˢ

Iſlãda
Roſmã

Mare Oceanuꝰ

Maria
Inſule
Beati Brandani
Branſiliæ
Dicte

Deſidate
inſule

Mare Oceanum

Beatæ inſule
fortune

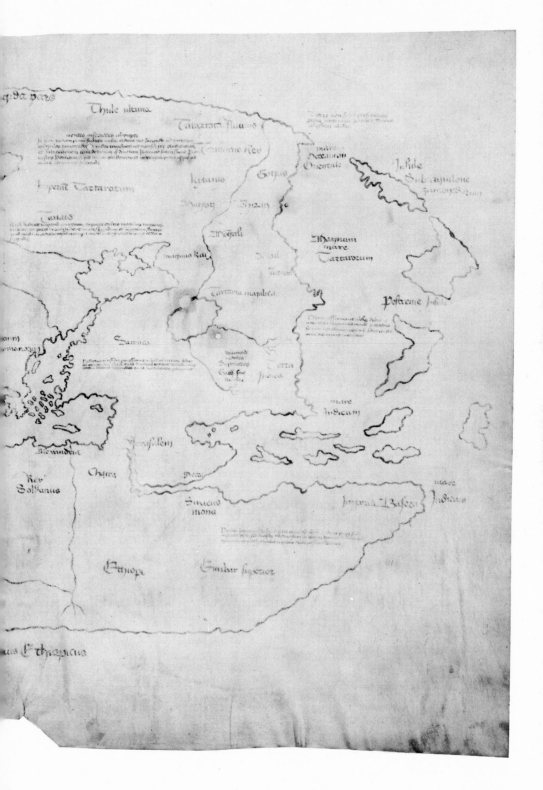

But for the moment, at least—and always keeping in mind that new facts might some day be uncovered to prove the map a fraud—probably the wisest course would be to accept the experts' opinion.

According to the story that the scholars have pieced together, the Vinland Map was drawn by a monk in Basel, Switzerland, during an important church council that was held there between 1431 and 1439. It was made to be part of a book called *Speculum Historicale* or, in English, *Mirror of History.*

Mirror of History was an attempt to tell the entire history of the world from the Creation to the crusade of Louis IX of France. It was written by a Norman monk, Vincent de Beauvais (1190–1264), and consisted of thirty-one books divided into 3,793 chapters. Such an ambitious work would need ambitious illustration. And our anonymous map-maker tried to fill this need by providing a map of the entire world.

Somehow, the map had not only been bound with *Mirror of History,* but also with a much shorter work, *Tartar Relation,* a thirty-two-page discussion of the Mongol peoples of Asia. All three works, in other words the map, *Tartar Relation,* and the enormous *Mirror of History,* were bound together.

Then, in the nineteenth century, something else happened. The map and *Tartar Relation* became separated from *Mirror of History* and were rebound together. In the year 1957, an American dealer in rare books purchased *Tartar Relation* along with the map and sold this portion to Yale University.

As I have said, the map attempts to be a representation of the entire world. There is nothing too remarkable in this, nor—for that matter—in the main body of the map itself. The representation of Europe is hardly error-free—though it is easily recognized. Asia and Africa were less successfully drawn than Europe.

It is not until we examine the upper left-hand section of the map that we can see what all the fuss was about. There, Iceland is portrayed (nothing remarkable about that either, by the way) and to the west of Iceland is a strikingly accurate drawing of Greenland labeled "Gronelada." To the west of Greenland is drawn an oddly shaped island called "Vinlanda," the Latin version of "Vinland." This is remarkable. For Vinland is a name that is very familiar to readers of the sagas, those tales of blood, history, and fantasy composed in Iceland from the end of the twelfth century through the first half of the fourteenth.

The sagas describe Vinland as an island southwest of Greenland. For many years, students of the Vikings have believed that there actually was a Vinland, and that it was located either on the North American continent or on an island close to its shores.

But just how factual are the sagas?

The answer to that one depends upon which sagas we have in mind. The Icelanders wrote a great number of them. Some appear to be pure fairy tales, complete with ghosts and trolls. Others are down-to-earth political history books, such as the *Islendinga Saga*, a detailed account of Iceland which begins with the year 1183, and covers much of the thirteenth century.

The "Saga of Eric the Red" and the "Greenlanders' Saga" are the ones which discuss Vinland or "Wineland." They appear to fall between the two extremes; they may not be as trustworthy as the political-historical sagas, but they do not have the "feel" of fairy tales. Their details may be wrong (as we shall see, they contradict each other on many details) but—according to those who believe that the Vikings were here before Columbus—their main outlines are true.

The proponents of the pre-Columbian Viking theory seized upon the Vinland Map as proof that they were right all along. Not only does the map show a Vinland, but it bears a legend stating in part that "the companions Bjarni [the Bjarni Herjolfsson of the sagas who is discussed in the next chapter] and Leif Eriksson discovered a new land, extremely fertile and even having vines." The saga story, it seemed, did have a basis in fact.

Or did it? The anti-map and anti-saga forces were quick to mount a counterattack. Greenland, they conceded, was rendered accurately. The accuracy was so great, indeed, as to be highly suspicious.

How could the Vikings, they wondered darkly, have had such a detailed knowledge of the ice-bound northern portions of that island? Vinland, on the other hand, was portrayed as an island—and such an island as had probably never existed on this earth. The shape is like a nightmare drawing of a monster amoeba. The island is divided into three sections by two great bodies of water, the northernmost one connecting the ocean with what looks to be a huge lake or bay.

But, while they are forced to admit that this island indeed has an odd shape, the pro-Vikings still insist that it was probably based on an earlier drawing of North America as the Scandinavians knew it. The northeast section of this continent does have two great waterways—the Gulf of St. Lawrence and the Hudson Strait. And the northernmost of these, Hudson Strait, leads to the great "inland sea" of Hudson Bay. The Vinland of the map, therefore, could well have been a rough sketch of eastern Canada conceived mistakenly as an island.

The fact that this sketch—and, of course, the earlier one that it was presumably based upon—is so rough should come as no surprise. The Vikings did not circumnavigate the Americas. They confined themselves to a comparatively small section of North America. And since they had come across only islands thus far in their westward explorations, it was logical for them to assume that this land, too, was an island.

Greenland was a different story. The Vikings stayed there a great deal longer—almost 430 years—and explored it much more thoroughly. And, even if it was difficult for them to examine the northernmost parts, it was not impossible. They could have mounted land expeditions, for example, during the mildest part of the summer. What was presumably the original map of Greenland probably would have been a lot more accurate than the one of Vinland, and the Vinland Map simply bears this out.

So far, the case for the Vikings—while not proved—begins to look better. But we have not yet concluded it. Two other maps have parts to play. One of these is by an Icelandic cartographer named Sigurd Stefansson who drew it in 1570 or 1590, though all we have now is a copy made in 1670. The other map was prepared by a Danish bishop, Hans Poulson Resen, in 1605.

Both of these maps were made well after Columbus's famous voyage in 1492. The two are extremely similar, one to the other, and were probably both based on a very early, pre-Columbian original. There are two reasons to believe this. First, Bishop Resen claims to have based his work on a map that was then several centuries old—in other words, one which had been drawn in pre-Columbian days. Second, both the bishop's map and Stefansson's map show details of the North American coastline which were not generally known at the time when the maps were drawn.

One explanation for what seems like an impossibility is that details of the coastline which had once been known were later forgotten. Both map-makers, in other words, used information which had been gathered by the old Norse explorers and then had dropped out of general circulation until its rediscovery during the seventeenth century. Another might be that Resen copied Stefansson who based his own map on the older one which Resen, too, was likely to have heard about.

In both maps the same major error is made. Greenland—though given a fairly recognizable shape—is shown as a peninsula attached to North America. Southwest of Greenland, on the Stefansson map, come the place-names of Helluland, Markland, and Skralinge Land, all of which are mentioned in the sagas. Bishop Resen has a slightly different arrangement of place-names. But below Markland in both maps is a finger of land which both map-makers called "Promontorium Winlandiae."

Now, here's the odd part. When we examine Stefansson's map from Helluland through Skralinge Land—deliberately ignoring both Gronlandia and Winlandiae—we find that it corresponds amazingly well to a modern map of Labrador. And where is Labrador? Its

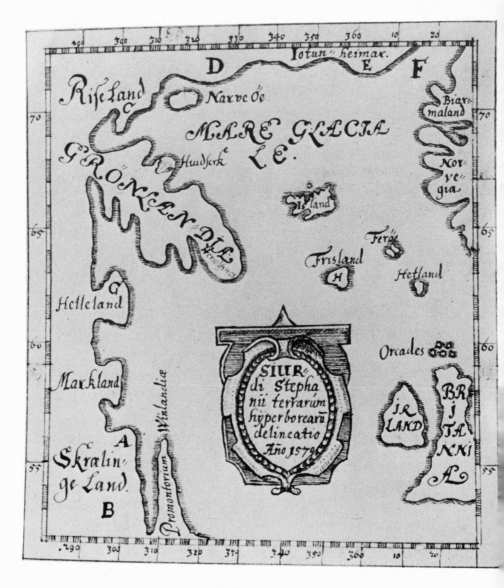

Stefansson's map.

coastline stretches from the Hudson Strait to the Gulf of St. Lawrence, those two great waterways which the pro-Viking scholars find on the Vinland Map.

Stefansson and Resen, however, drew Greenland as a peninsula. Why this discrepancy?

We simply do not know. One reasonable explanation is that the early cartographer who made the map that both Stefansson and Resen followed did not have all the information that the Vinland Map maker had. Perhaps he drew his before the northernmost section of Greenland was explored. Or perhaps he had poorer sources than the other cartographer. At any rate, while making southern Greenland reasonably true to shape, he attached the northern part of the island to the continent.

Promontorium Winlandiae—or the Promontory of Vinland—is here joined to the North American mainland. This is probably a mistake. It should have been joined to the island of Newfoundland.

Newfoundland is located in the right position—in the mouth of the Gulf of St. Lawrence. The northeastern peninsula of the island comes very close to the mainland but is separated from it by the narrow Strait of Belle Isle. The map-maker merely joined the peninsula to the continent instead of to the island.

There is evidence from archaeology that Vinland really was attached to Newfoundland's northeastern peninsula.

In 1961, Dr. Helge Ingstad located what he believes to be the remains of an old Viking camp at the Newfoundland site of L'Anse-aux-Meadows by the Strait of Belle Isle. Among the artifacts that Dr. Ingstad found there was an old spindle whorl, which indicates that women as well as men lived at the camp. Since Norsemen did not bring their women along unless they intended to settle, and the sagas indicate that it was decided to settle Vinland, we can infer that this site was indeed Vinland.

There are still some who doubt Dr. Ingstad's findings. The artifacts are so worn with age, they point out, that they can't be identified as Norse with any real certainty. Perhaps it is the abandoned remains of an early French camp that might have been pitched there around the seventeenth century.

Dr. Ingstad replied by having the artifacts dated by means of the carbon-14 method. But even though the dates checked out, that did not still the cries of the skeptics who reason that carbon-14 dating is not all that accurate either.

And there—for now, at least—the case for the Vikings must rest. We have the evidence of the sagas, of the three maps, and of Dr. Ingstad's site at L'Anse-aux-Meadows.

How does the case stand up? You must decide for yourself. But it seems to me that, while any one of these pieces of evidence might be considered shaky if standing alone, they all fit together too neatly to be shrugged off.

The Vikings, then, were probably here. But where? Did they visit any other parts of our continent? Or did they stay in Newfoundland and perhaps along the shores of Labrador? There is some evidence that they did explore further. For now, though, let's return to Greenland and the westward push towards the place that the Norsemen thought of as "Vinland the Good."

VII.
Vinland

Even though the end of the Greenland colony was both tragic and pathetic, no one can deny the glory of its beginning. The men and women who came to Greenland in those early days were among the most fascinating of all the Viking people.

We have already met the colony's founder, Eric the Red, a man who seems to have combined wisdom and combativeness in almost equal amounts. We will soon take a closer look at Eric's son, Leif, who was even more remarkable than his father.

Now, however, we are going to meet another father and son combination from the sagas: Herjolf Bardsson and his son, Bjarni.

Herjolf must have been a good man to know. A descendant of Aud the Deep-Minded, he was a member of the ruling class of Iceland. Like many of that class, he made his own living as a merchant sea captain and trader.

Bjarni Herjolfsson was also bred to the sea. Even as a youth, the sagas tell us, he showed much promise. As he grew to maturity, he prospered both in material wealth and in public esteem. Before too long, Bjarni had his own ship and was in business for himself. Herjolf quit the sea soon after and retired to his farm on Iceland. Bjarni would spend every second winter with his parents—leaving in the springtime in order to go off on an extended trading voyage. He would spend that winter in Norway and not return to Iceland until the following year.

One of the periods which Bjarni spent in Europe was the winter of 984–985. You may recall that it was in the spring of 985 that Eric the Red was trying to find Icelanders who were willing to settle on Greenland with him. It is doubtful that many of these pioneers were of more than middle age. Most of those answering Eric's call to adventure were likely to have been younger men and women anxious to leave the homes of their parents and make new lives on their own.

But there was at least one man among that original group of Greenland settlers who was around sixty years old. That was Herjolf Bardsson.

No one can say what it was that made Herjolf decide to leave what must have been a comfortable and rewarding life on Iceland in order to sail off with his wife to whatever hardships awaited him in Greenland. On the face of it, it seems improbable that he would wish to do so. Yet sail he did.

Bjarni—who was in his mid-thirties at the time—was away from Iceland when his father left with Eric. When he returned home to find his parents gone, he was understandably upset. On hearing the news, he did not even bother to unload his ship's cargo, but began immediate preparations to fit the vessel out for sea once more.

These preparations took his crew by surprise and they asked Bjarni what he had in mind. It was his custom, Bjarni explained, to spend alternate winters with his father. If his shipmates were willing to go with him, therefore, he would take the ship to Greenland. To a man, the crew agreed. But Bjarni was too fair and prudent a person to let it go at that. He insisted on giving his men one more chance to back out.

"None of us has ever sailed the Greenland Sea before," he

warned. "This voyage must be considered a foolhardy one."

Still Bjarni's men remained faithful. As soon as the knarr was ready, they pulled it out of the safe harbors of Iceland and steered for Greenland.

Bjarni's warning to his crew was a realistic one. It was foolhardy to attempt the trip to Greenland without either charts or the advice of someone who had made the crossing before.

All that Bjarni really knew was that, somewhere to the west of Iceland, was a land of mountains and glaciers. He headed his ship's prow in a westerly direction. But when gales sprang up to push the craft to the south, he had no way of knowing how far off-course he was—or even if he was off-course at all. Even then, however, he might have figured it out—but a fog arose and completely surrounded the ship.

It is not easy for us today to put ourselves in Bjarni Herjolfsson's place. He was utterly helpless. He had no radar, no sonar, no compass, no radio with which to call for help. His entire universe was confined to a small open boat, and the only aid he could look for was his own skill and the skill of his companions.

Many days passed this way—with the knarr lost and fog-bound and the crew trying desperately to keep their courage up. Then at last the fog lifted. The Norsemen could take their bearings and hoist their sail. Heading westward again, the knarr sailed for one more day until the men spotted land.

Was this finally Greenland? Bjarni for one did not think so. This land was too flat and too heavily wooded to be Greenland. It must be some new land, he thought, which no Viking had yet set foot on.

There is not much doubt that this land of low hills and dense forests was some place on North America. Just which part of the American continent it was, however, is still a subject of debate. Some believe that Bjarni had drifted as far south as Cape Cod. Most experts, though, favor either Newfoundland or possibly Labrador.

Whatever part of America this was, Bjarni refused to land on it. He was not an adventurer by trade, after all, but a responsible merchant captain who could well imagine the dangers that he and his men might meet on an unknown shore. Although his men might have grumbled, Bjarni was determinedly prudent. Figuring that he must now be south of Greenland, he headed back to sea in a northerly direction.

After two more days of sailing, Bjarni made another sighting. This section of land was also heavily wooded. It was flatter than the first place, however. Indeed, it had no hills at all.

Where was he this time? Those who believe that Bjarni's first sighting was at Cape Cod are sure that this second landfall was someplace on Nova Scotia. The more accepted view is that he was now near Cape Porcupine on the southeastern coast of Labrador.

By now the men were disgusted with Bjarni's single-minded policy of refusing to land until they reached Greenland. They had already spent too many days cooped up on their little knarr and were itching to go ashore. But this did not make any sense to Bjarni. There was still plenty of food and water aboard the ship. What purpose would there be in disembarking here?

So once more the captain ordered his vessel to put out to sea. And after three days of further sailing it came once more to a new land. This time the land was probably one of the small islands off Baffin Island—Loks Land perhaps, or Resolution Island.

This third land was rocky and had "mountains of ice" (probably glaciers) on it. But it did not fit the descriptions of Greenland which Bjarni had locked in his memory.

As for the crew, they were still anxious to go exploring. But Bjarni was more adamant than ever. This land certainly had nothing to recommend it, he said. Despite the mutterings of the men, therefore, the knarr did not lower its sails.

By now Bjarni must have realized that he had passed by Greenland altogether, for he changed course and headed the ship back in an easterly direction. In four more days he sighted land again.

He examined the shoreline carefully. From everything he had heard about Greenland, this could well be it.

"Here," he announced at last, "we shall steer to the land."

This time Bjarni had what can only be described as a truly amazing stroke of luck. For he had not only reached Greenland, but—by a wild coincidence—the very cape where his father had his farm.

Once Bjarni was reunited with his father, he decided to change his style of life. He gave up the career of merchant captain and went to live on Herjolf's Greenland estate, which he took over and ran after the older man died.

Some time later, though, Bjarni did visit Europe again. There he stayed for a while at the court of Earl Eric Hakonarson, who controlled Norway from 1000 to 1014.

The earl, we are told, was very interested in Bjarni's experiences. There were some people at the court, however, who publicly wondered how anyone could have been quite so lacking in imagination as to refrain from exploring unknown lands.

It is a puzzle which still nags at us today. From everything we know about Bjarni, he was no coward, but a shrewd and competent sea captain. Why did he refuse to at least send out a shore party to do some preliminary exploration? It seems like a most un-Viking way to behave.

The answer may well lie in Bjarni's single-minded desire to join his parents on Greenland. He was not making this trip for the fun of it, after all. He was a man with a purpose. And he was not going to permit himself to be sidetracked from his purpose simply to explore a new land.

The famous Viking who seized the chance that Bjarni passed up was Eric the Red's son, Leif.

There are two different versions of how this came about. One version is told in "Eric the Red's Saga," while the other may be found in the "Greenlanders' Saga."

Why these two sagas disagree—and, as we shall see, they become much more contradictory later on—has remained unanswered to this day. They were obviously written down by two different people with two different versions of events. And, as the sagas were probably first recited by poets and passed down orally from generation to generation long before they were put on paper, "Eric the Red's Saga" and the "Greenlanders' Saga" must have sprung from two different oral traditions—both perhaps a century or two old.

Why should they vary so? One reason could be that they originated among members of different families. The Icelanders considered the men and women of the sagas to be their forebears. It would be quite normal for each family or clan to wish to give its own ancestors a more prominent place. In the same way, when a person is made out to be a villain or villainess in one of the sagas, it might indicate that the family of the author was having a feud with the "villain's" descendants.

But this is pure speculation. All we know for certain is that these two sagas differ from each other.

According to "Eric the Red's Saga," Leif's achievement was one of those fortunate accidents which do happen from time to time. When Leif was in Norway he served at the court of King Olaf Tryggvesson, the great Christianizing king who ruled that country from 995 to 1000—or just before Earl Eric Hakonarson came to power. King Olaf had apparently converted Leif to the new faith. Now he wanted him to return home in order to convert the Greenlanders.

Leif did his best to refuse this assignment. As the son of Eric the Red, he must have been only too well aware of how stubborn his fellow Vikings would be, and he did not underestimate the problems he would encounter in carrying out King Olaf's request. But the king somehow finally got Leif to go.

On the way back to Greenland, Leif's ship was blown off its course by a storm. He and his crew landed on new shores, where they found vines, maple trees, and a wild cereal, possibly wild rice, growing in the fields. He gathered samples of these items and headed back home with news of his discovery.

He was nearly at his destination when he rescued some ship-wrecked men and then converted them to Christianity. It was that incident which earned him the title of "Leif the Lucky."

This, at any rate, is the story recorded in "Eric the Red's Saga." The "Greenlanders' Saga" gives us a very different—and to many people a far more logical—sequence of events.

In the "Greenlanders' " version, we are told that there was a great deal of talk on Greenland about the new lands which Bjarni had seen. One man in that settlement who decided to do more than talk was Leif Eriksson.

Leif first of all paid a visit to Bjarni Herjolfsson who would have been the one man best equipped to advise him as to routes and other details of the voyage. He bought Bjarni's ship and hired a crew of thirty-five seamen.

Leif's plan was to have his father take over as leader of the expedition. But Eric resisted this suggestion. He was too old for exploration now, he felt, and was not at all sure that he could endure the hardships of a long sea voyage.

Still Leif kept pressing him. Eric the Red, the great discoverer of Greenland, would be certain to bring good luck with him. And a journey to Bjarni's lands would need all the luck it could get.

Eric finally consented to take charge. When the ship was ready to sail, he and his son set out on horseback to reach the place where it rode at anchor. They were almost there when Eric's horse stumbled and threw him so that the older man injured his foot.

It was apparently not a very serious injury. But Eric took it as a sign from the fates that he should stay at home.

"It is not meant for me to discover more lands than the one in which we live," he told his son. "We can continue together no longer."

Eric had made up his mind. He returned to Brattahlid alone, leaving Leif to head up the expedition.

Leif Eriksson charted a course that was the exact opposite of the one that Bjarni followed by chance. After his discussions with his fellow Viking, he was able to head directly for the third land which Bjarni had seen.

When he reached this land, he recognized it at once. There was no grass there, but flat rock that stretched all the way from the sea to the great ice mountains. Bjarni was right, Leif decided. The land had no good qualities. But Leif and his men had explored it for themselves.

"It hasn't happened with us as it did with Bjarni," Leif remarked then. "People cannot say that we did not set foot upon it."

Leif formally named this land *Helluland*—or Flat Stone Country. He then ordered his men back to the ship so they could start on their way to Bjarni's second land.

This too they found with little or no trouble. And as Bjarni had said, it was both level and heavily wooded. They landed on a broad sandy beach and spent some time in exploration before returning to their vessel once more and setting sail.

Before they left, however, Leif also gave this land a suitable name. He called it *Markland*—or Forest Country.

The third land that Leif came to—Bjarni's first land, he thought —may have been the northern tip of Newfoundland by the L'Anse-aux-Meadows side where the remains of what appear to be old Norse dwellings (see Chapter VI) were found in 1961.

First, though, he stopped at a small offshore island where he and his men went briefly ashore. It happened to be a beautiful day and there was dew on the grass. Leif and the others touched the dew and placed their fingers to their mouths. They could not remember having ever tasted anything as sweet as this, the saga tells us.

They took this as a good omen, and they must have been in high spirits as they left the island and sailed into a sound of what they believed to be the mainland. The tide was at the ebb now. They passed a cape and ran the knarr aground in shallow water. They were still some distance from the shore, but they were so anxious to

"Markland." This location, known from the Icelandic sagas, can be identified as Cape Porcupine and The Strand on the Coast of Labrador. Leif found the country here "flat and covered with forest, with extensive white sands wherever they went, and shelving gently to the sea." Two days later, to the south, Vinland was sighted.

set foot on land that they did not wait for the ship to float but rowed there in a longboat.

They found a stream there that was fed from a lake and emptied into the sound. As soon as the tide was high enough, they rowed back to the ship and took it into the lake, where they anchored it.

Artist's conception of Leif Eriksson's ship sailing into the American shores. Painting by Arbo.

The men moved off their ship now and threw up some small shelters so that they could live comfortably ashore. This was a beautiful land. The fishing there was marvelous, with salmon especially bountiful. The men swore that they had never seen such large salmon in their lives.

With fall approaching, the men built some larger houses so that they could stay there for the winter.

It turned out to be a pleasant winter. With the climate generally warmer in that area than it is today, there was little frost and the grass hardly turned brown. The grass remained so fresh, indeed, that they thought that cattle would need little fodder even in winter.

Once the houses were finished, Leif divided his men into two parties, one to remain at the main encampment and the other to explore the countryside. Leif himself spent alternate days exploring and staying at home.

He did issue a set of strict orders to the exploring parties, however. They were never to wander so far from home base that they could not get back that same evening. And under no circumstances were the men to get separated from each other. On one expedition, though, these safety precautions were disobeyed. A man named Tyrker became separated from the rest.

Leif had spent that day at home. When he saw the exploring party return without Tyrker he was furious. He would not have wanted to lose any of his men, of course, but Tyrker the German was a very special one. An older man, he had been a long-time

Discovery of America by Leif Eriksson, *as conceived by the painter Clyde Deland.*

friend of Eric the Red's and had been like a second father to Leif when Leif was a boy.

Without loss of time Leif organized a search party of twelve men. They had hardly left the area of the houses when they spotted Tyrker.

The German was brimming over with news. He was so excited by what he had to tell that it took him a while to remember to speak in Norse and not in his native language.

"I have something to report," the men finally understood him to say. "Although I did not walk much farther than you, I have found vines and grapes!"

Leif wondered whether this could be possible. "Is that really true, foster father?"

Tyrker assured him that it was true. He had been born in wine country. He knew grapevines when he saw them.

To understand why this find should have been so exciting to Leif and the other Vikings, we have to remember that the Norse exploration trips were never only for adventure or to satisfy curiosity, although these motives did play an important part. There was always a commercial purpose for the Viking journeys. The Norsemen were ever hopeful of finding cargo to take home and sell at a profit.

So far Leif had found a plentiful supply of good timber—something that was much in demand in Greenland. But grapes and grapevines were also very profitable. Leif now knew that he would be able to carry back a varied cargo of timber, vines, and grapes.

During the rest of the winter, the men were busy chopping and stripping trees, gathering grapes and cutting the vines. When spring came, a full cargo was ready to be loaded aboard Leif's ship.

Before he set sail, however, Leif decided to name this country as he had the two other lands that he had explored earlier. He called it *Vinland*—or Wine Land.

The voyage home passed without incident until the men were once more within sight of Greenland. That was when Leif spotted a boat that had foundered on a reef. He was able to rescue fifteen people from the boat and was afterwards known as "Leif the Lucky."

As we have seen, the two versions of Leif's journey to the New World quite thoroughly contradict each other. Which are we to believe—the tale as told in "Eric the Red's Saga" or the more complicated version which I have just extracted from the "Greenlanders' Saga"?

In the end everyone will have to make his own choice. There is no real proof that the details of either story are more accurate. For myself, though, I tend to go along with the "Greenlanders' " version. It makes more sense to me. It has a more logical ring. The story of Leif setting out from Norway to Greenland as a religious missionary and then being blown across the sea to a beautiful new land seems just a little too good to be true.

The question of which version to believe may become a little clearer when we recall that Bjarni Herjolfsson's earlier voyage was not mentioned at all in "Eric the Red's Saga." Perhaps the circumstance of Bjarni's missing Greenland and stumbling on the New World through a combination of fog and storm (unlike Leif, remember, Bjarni had only the vaguest idea of how to reach Greenland) was mistakenly ascribed to Leif Eriksson by the author of this saga. As for the notion of Leif's being a Christian missionary from Norway at this stage of his career, that might well have been put in in order to lend prestige to the Church by involving it in Leif's discovery.

Once we concede that Bjarni sighted the New World first, the version related in the "Greenlanders' Saga" becomes even more likely.

At the time we are talking about, the relatively few people on Greenland were all confined to the original Eastern Settlement. When Bjarni arrived with his exciting news of unknown lands, that had to have been the main topic of conversation throughout the settlement. Of course the Greenlanders would discuss going to those places themselves—both to explore and hopefully to make a profit.

To a Viking who actually planned to mount such a trip of exploration, the next moves would seem obvious. He would talk to Bjarni
first and get whatever advice he could from him. Then, if he had the
money to do it, he would probably purchase Bjarni's boat—which
had already proved itself to be a lucky craft in the minds of the superstitious Vikings by making the voyage safely. This is exactly
what the "Greenlanders' Saga" says Leif did.

To further pinpoint a likely sequence of events, let's take a closer
look at Leif's next action. Now that he had Bjarni's lucky boat, he
tried to get his father to lead the expedition because of the luck that
Eric the Red would bring.

This was perfectly reasonable according to the Norse way of
thinking. Luck had an almost mystical meaning for the Vikings. But
Eric's luck was a pagan luck. If Leif were a devout Christian, he
would not have agreed to take advantage of a pagan's luck—even if
the pagan happened to be his father.

At the time of the Vinland expedition, therefore, Leif was probably still a pagan. He made his plans as prudently and carefully as he
could and then went off on his journey, which turned out to be an
extremely profitable one.

It was after this—when he was already well known as the discoverer of Vinland—that he served at the court of King Olaf of Norway who personally converted him to Christianity.

It would have been an intelligent move on the king's part, then, to
have ordered Leif back to Greenland as a missionary. Who could
have been more effective in this role, after all, than a recent convert
who was not merely the son of the colony's founder but a great hero
in his own right?

Bjarni must have made his own state visit to Norway at a later
date—after King Olaf had died. No wonder the people at the court
of Earl Eric talked about his lack of imagination. They were probably comparing him with Leif Eriksson.

As contradictory as the two versions of Leif's discovery are, they
do agree on some things. First, they agree that Leif and his men

were the first Vikings to actually walk the shores of the New World. They both state that, on his way home, he found some ship-wrecked men, rescued them, and thus earned his nickname of "Leif the Lucky." Both sagas mention vines and grapes.

Here we run into some difficulty. It happens to be an awkward fact that grapes simply will not grow on the eastern coast of North America above a point twenty miles or so south of Boston.

If we were to locate Vinland someplace on Cape Cod (that used to be the most commonly held view) there would be no problem.

L'Anse-aux-Meadows, site of the Viking settlement, showing excavations of the Long House.

Grapes will grow on Cape Cod. But most everything else—including the archaeological evidence—points to the L'Anse-aux-Meadows site on Newfoundland as the location of Leif Eriksson's main camp. And Newfoundland is much too far north to support grapes.

Fortunately, there are two ways out of this dilemma.

First, although it is true that grapes won't grow beyond a certain point on the American northeast coast *today,* during the Viking period the climate was generally warmer there than it is now. It might have been warm enough for wild grapes to thrive on Newfoundland. In fact, long after the end of the Viking era there were reports of wild grapes growing in different parts of Canada. One of these re-

Excavations of the Sauna Bath at L'Anse-aux-Meadows.

ports comes from Jacques Cartier, the French navigator who sailed down the west coat of Newfoundland in 1534 and discovered the St. Lawrence River the following year. Cartier claimed to have found grapes growing on the Ile d'Orleans, just downriver from Quebec. It is true that Quebec is both inland and farther south than Newfoundland. But even closer to our own time than this—in the 1660's—a British surgeon named James Yonge described wild grapes growing on the same Newfoundland peninsula that shelters the L'Anse-aux-Meadows site. Apparently, therefore, grapes could have grown at L'Anse-aux-Meadows when Leif was there.

The second way out of this dilemma comes from our knowledge of the Norse language. It was not absolutely necessary for those "grapes" to have been grapes at all. The Norse words which we ordinarily translate as vines and grapes could have actually meant vines and wine-berries.

A great variety of berries still grows in the area of the L'Anse-aux-Meadows site. Among the types now there that can be made into wine are blueberries, blackberries, currants (which are known as "wine-berries" in parts of England and Scotland), gooseberries, and squashberries. Squashberries are particularly intriguing as they are red in color, quite tasty, and grow on bushes in almost grapelike clusters.

The berry situation is far different on Greenland, incidentally, where the only ones to be found are whortleberries, blueberries, and cranberries. Importing different kinds of wine-making berries to the Greenland colony, therefore, would probably have been most profitable.

But did the Norse know how to make wine from berries around the year 1000? We cannot tell for sure—but we do know that they had this skill less than two hundred years later. Norway's King Sverre, who ruled from 1177 to 1202, once even suggested using wild berry wine as altar wine instead of the variety made from grapes. It is highly probable that the early Greenland Vikings could also make wild berry wine.

Whether Leif took a cargo of valuable berries back to Greenland, or whether he carried back the grapes which might also have grown wild at L'Anse-aux-Meadows, that site remains the best bet for his "country" of Vinland. The land there was so fertile, and his voyage there so profitable, that it soon became known as "Vinland the Good."

VIII.
The "Wretches"

What sort of man was Leif Eriksson, this explorer whom the sagas claim was the first Norseman to tread the shore of North America? His character seems to have been an admirable one. He had obviously inherited his father's courage as well as his shrewdness. But, far beyond that, Leif comes through as a wise and thoughtful leader with a strong sense of justice and a real concern for the welfare of his men.

There are many Vikings who are fun to read about. But Leif appears to have been one of the few whom we might have wished to have known in person.

Although Leif Eriksson was by far the most famous of Eric the Red's children, three more of Eric's children were to play important roles in the Norse discovery and exploration of the New World as recorded in the sagas.

One of these children was Leif's younger brother, Thorvald Eriksson.

When Leif returned to Greenland to report his experiences across the sea, Thorvald commented that the new land had not yet been sufficiently explored. Thorvald wanted to finish the job that Leif had started. He also had a more long-range plan in mind—one which we will soon discover.

Leif must have smiled tolerantly at Thorvald's ambitions. If his brother wished to lead an expedition to Vinland, he would let him have his own ship—the same vessel that was purchased from Bjarni. This was a generous offer, and one which Thorvald was quick to accept. According to the "Greenlanders' Saga"—which is the only source we have for the events on this voyage—Thorvald began making preparations immediately to leave Greenland. Following Leif's advice, he rounded up a crew of thirty men.

Thorvald seems to have had no trouble in charting a direct course to Vinland. There he found Leifsbudir—the houses that Leif had built when he was there. The houses were still in good condition, so Thorvald's men used them all during the winter. Like Leif before them, they were able to catch enough fish to feed themselves well during the cold months.

As soon as spring came, the men set sail in order to explore the western coast of what must have been the island of Newfoundland. They discovered a series of lovely beaches and numerous forests, but with a single exception saw no traces of either animals or human beings. The exception was a wooden grain bin which they spotted on one of the offshore islands.

They returned to Leifsbudir in the autumn and spent a second winter there. When the days lengthened again, they resumed their investigations—this time sailing north and east.

This extra-careful inspection that Thorvald was making of Vinland and the surrounding country gives us a clue to the long-range plan which must have been in the back of his mind. It reminds us of the close inspection that his father, Eric the Red, once made of Greenland, and Thorvald's purpose was probably much the same. He wanted to learn whether it would be possible to make a permanent colony in Vinland, and not use it only as a base for all-male expeditions.

Thus far, he must have been encouraged. Thorvald liked this country; even when his ship went aground off a cape and its keel was severely damaged, he and his men kept their spirits up. They repaired the keel, named the cape Keelness in its honor, and went on their way.

They continued exploring the shoreline until they sailed into a bay which had a small finger of land jutting into it. They anchored there and went ashore.

"This is a fair land," Thorvald mused then. "I would like to make my home here."

But Thorvald was due for an unpleasant surprise. The country had natives in it. On returning to their ship, Thorvald and his men spotted three overturned skin-canoes on the beach. Three men were hiding under each canoe. A fight quickly followed—apparently the first fight in which the Norse took part on these shores.

Who were the natives? The Norsemen called them *Skraelings,* a Viking term of contempt which may be translated as "wretches." They had to have been either American Indians or Eskimos. The fact that they were encountered on a northern trip makes us think of Eskimos. So do their skin-boats, as the Indian canoe was made out of birch bark and not skin.

Although this is not proof positive (the first descriptions we have of Indian bark canoes were written several hundred years later; the Indians might have been using skin-canoes during the Viking era) the probability is that these northern natives were Eskimos. Other Norsemen were to meet with Indians later on, on journeys to the south. To the Vikings, however, all the natives seemed the same. They were all ugly Skraelings.

In their first fight with the Skraelings, the Norsemen captured all but one man who managed to escape in his canoe. The Vikings killed their prisoners and went to sleep undoubtedly well pleased with themselves.

Although this may have been a satisfactory day's work for Thorvald and his men, it was not satisfactory for others of the "wretches" who must have been warned by the man who got away. The Norsemen were still sleeping off their victory when a battery of skin-boats came up the bay to attack the Viking ship.

Realizing that he was outnumbered, Thorvald took a defensive position. He ordered protective boards up on both sides of the ship to serve as breastworks and warned his men to keep behind them.

"We must defend ourselves to the best of our ability," he said. "But offer little attack."

The strategy worked. The natives shot arrows at the ship for a while, then retreated.

When the battle was over, Thorvald first checked his men to see if there were any wounded among them. When it turned out that there weren't, he admitted that he had taken an arrow in his armpit.

Thorvald showed them the shaft of the arrow, and told them that this would mean his death. He advised the men to return to Leifsbudir as quickly as possible. But before they set sail, he wanted to be buried on that headland he had thought was so beautiful.

"Perhaps I was speaking the truth before," he said, "when I wished to make my home there."

The men buried Thorvald, according to his final instructions, with a cross at his head and another at his feet. Following his wishes, they named that place Crossness and sailed sadly back to their Vinland headquarters.

They spent the winter on Vinland, loaded the ship with grapes and timber, and sailed back to Greenland with their cargo the following spring. They landed at Ericsfjord, near Brattahlid, and told Leif the story of what happened.

"Eric the Red's Saga" and the "Greenlanders' Saga" both agree that the next expedition to the New World was an ill-fated one under the command of Thorstein Eriksson, another of the sons of

Eric the Red. As in the case of Leif's original voyage, the two sagas differ greatly in details.

"Eric the Red's Saga," as we have seen, does not record the journey of Thorvald Eriksson at all. It does have Thorvald dying as the result of an arrow wound, but on another expedition under the leadership of somebody else.

This saga takes up the story of Thorstein after Leif's return from his Vinland voyage. It states that Thorstein—whom the author describes as good, wise, and having many friends—then set out to explore the land which Leif had discovered. It is interesting to note that the incident of Eric's son begging him to take charge of the voyage, and the older man reluctantly agreeing until he is thrown from his horse on the way to the ship, is recounted here in "Eric the Red's Saga." But the son, naturally, is Thorstein instead of Leif.

According to this source, Thorstein started out with a crew of twenty men. In the beginning everyone was in good spirits. But storms came up and tossed the men about on the ocean so that they never could get back on the right course to Vinland.

As a matter of fact, the vessel was carried in the opposite direction. On one occasion it came within sight of Iceland. On another the men were somewhere off Ireland. Thorstein finally made it back to Ericsfjord in the autumn with both himself and his men in a state of near exhaustion. Afterwards, we are told, Thorstein married a woman named Gudrid. He died in Greenland shortly thereafter.

The "Greenlanders' Saga," on the other hand, sticks to its main thrust and takes up the tale with the return of Thorvald's crew. In this version Thorstein sets out on his journey with the express purpose of bringing home his brother's body. He is already married to Gudrid and takes her on the trip with him. This may well indicate that, like Thorvald before him, he was also thinking of future colonization. Thorstein and Gudrid took a crew of twenty-five men on the same vessel that Bjarni, Eric, and Thorvald had sailed to the New World.

The story is now much the same as in "Eric the Red's Saga." Storms drove them all over the ocean and they returned to Greenland totally worn out.

They landed at the Western Settlement, where Thorstein and Gudrid found a place to stay for the winter. But long before the warm weather set in again, Thorstein became sick and died, perhaps as a result of the hardships he suffered on his voyage.

Here again we are faced with the choice of which saga to believe.

I tend to favor the "Greenlanders' Saga" here. When taken together with the other Norse expeditions I think it sounds more consistent. If the Greenlanders were thinking about colonization, it seems logical that Thorstein would take his wife along to look over a possible new home. And of course a Viking would try to bring back the body of a slain brother.

But you must make your own decision.

As we have seen, there are many disagreements between the sagas. The biggest set of discrepancies of all concerns the New World experiences of Thorfinn Karlsefni's expedition.

Thorfinn Karlsefni was an Icelandic merchant who spent one winter visiting Leif Eriksson at Brattahlid on Greenland. It was there—and both sagas agree on this—that Karlsefni caught the Vinland bug.

The "Greenlanders' Saga" gives us another clue to Karlsefni's interest in exploration. He fell in love with Thorstein Eriksson's widow, Gudrid, and wished to marry her. He was marrying into a family tradition of New World exploration.

As the head of the family, Leif gave his permission for his sister-in-law to marry Karlsefni. The wedding was held that winter. In the coming spring, Karlsefni planned to take Gudrid—who had tried and failed to make the journey with her first husband—to Vinland.

This was going to be a far more impressive attempt than Thorstein's, however. Vinland had already been explored. Karlsefni and his wife were taking other women along so they could found a colony immediately on landing. To help with this effort, Leif agreed to lend the expedition his houses in Vinland.

When the expedition left Greenland, it had two other vessels in addition to Karlsefni's ship. One was also an Icelandic craft, commanded by Bjarni Grimolfsson and Thorhall Gamlasson. The other was captained by Thorvard of Gardar, a Greenland farmer who had married a girl named Freydis who was an illegitimate daughter of Eric the Red.

In the same ship with Thorvard and Freydis was an irrepressible old pagan, Thorhall the Hunter. And one of the two surviving manuscript versions of "Eric the Red's Saga" states that Thorvald Eriksson (whom the "Greenlanders' Saga" had already killed off in the New World) was also on Thorvard's ship.

According to "Eric the Red's Saga," a total of one hundred and sixty men and women plus provisions and livestock were aboard the two vessels. "Greenlanders' Saga," however, gives a more modest figure of sixty men and five women. The year this crossing was made is also in dispute. Modern experts estimate dates ranging from A.D. 1004 to A.D. 1020.

When the ships left Ericsfjord, they first sailed all the way up the coast of Greenland to the Western Settlement. Then they headed east to cross the Atlantic. Their route seems to have been rather a sentimental one, for it followed closely that of the earlier Viking expeditions. They stopped first at what they thought was Helluland, a place with many flat stones and inhabited by arctic foxes. From there they sailed south for two days until they reached what seemed to be Leif's Markland. After making a stop at Keelness, and investigating several unknown spots along the way, they finally arrived at what was to be their first headquarters in the New World.

Where was this? Here we come to the first really important disagreement between the sagas. According to the "Greenlanders' Saga," they had found Vinland, and settled into Leif's houses where they spent a pleasant winter. But "Eric the Red's Saga" is just as

The northern extremity of Vinland (Cape Bould), seen from the Strait of Belle Isle, New-

positive that they never reached Vinland at all, and spent a nasty winter at a place they named Straumsfjord.

Chances are that the "Greenlanders' Saga" is right. Leifsbudir— or Leif's houses—were probably located at the L'Anse-aux-Meadows site on Newfoundland. One object that was found in those old ruins was a spindle whorl—an item that was used by Norse women. It seems evident, therefore, that women were among those who stayed at Leifsbudir.

According to the "Greenlanders' Saga," it is true that another male-female expedition followed that of Thorfinn Karlsefni. But this voyage was led by Leif's half-sister, Freydis, who was there first with the Karlsefni expedition and then returned.

From this point on, the sagas differ so widely in their accounts that I am going to make a choice. Rather than try to give both versions, I will follow tradition by taking the basic story from "Eric the Red's Saga." I will combine that, however, with those sections of the "Greenlanders' Saga" that seem most likely to be true.

Because "Greenlanders' Saga" says that the Vikings probably did spend the winter at Leifsbudir, we can believe (as "Eric the Red's Saga" states) that they had a rugged time of it. Climate does vary

foundland. The area where Leif and Karlsefni settled can be glimpsed in the distance (right).

from year to year. Leif and Thorvald Eriksson had such good winter weather during their separate stays that this winter was probably due for a change.

Although the Karlsefni expedition did manage to save its livestock, both the hunting and the fishing failed. There were times when the Norsemen were on a very restricted diet indeed.

The one joyful event which did take place during the cold months occurred in the fall. This was the birth of Gudrid and Karlsefni's first child, a boy named Snorri. Snorri Karlsefnisson was the first child on record to have been born in America of European ancestry. He survived his experiences here to return to Iceland with his parents. After Karlsefni's death in Iceland, Snorri took over his father's farm, married, and had children of his own.

When spring came to Vinland, and food became plentiful once more, Karlsefni decided to investigate the country to the south. Thorhall the Hunter did not agree, but with nine other men he took one of the ships to survey the north, while the rest of the Vikings joined Karlsefni in his southerly explorations.

It is not known how far south the main body of Norsemen managed to get. They did sail for a long time, however, before they finally entered a bay that was fed by a river. The sea entrance to the bay was protected by sandbars, so a ship could enter the harbor only during high tide. The Vikings named this place Hop—a Norse word meaning lake or bay.

The Vikings landed at Hop and decided to settle there, at least for a while. They found it to be a lovely place with an abundance of grapevines and a wild cereal which may have been wild rice. There were also many game animals in the woods around Hop, while the waters there were teeming with fish. The Norsemen dug trenches along the shore at the high-water marks. When the tide rose, the trenches filled with water, leaving large numbers of halibut trapped when the ocean receded again.

The Vikings lived this way for two weeks before they were visited by Skraelings, the natives in skin-boats. The visitors stayed offshore and waved sticks that made an odd rattling sound. The Norsemen were unsure of their visitors' intentions, but one of the Vikings suggested that the noisy sticks might be a sign of peace. Hoping that this was the case, the Vikings raised a white shield which apparently satisfied the natives, who then came ashore. The Skraelings stood there for a while marveling at the Norsemen, who in turn marveled at them. At last the natives went away.

It is possible that the explorers—or perhaps the author of the saga —were mistaken about the skin-boats, for these southerly skraelings were very likely to have been Indians.

Not only did the encounter probably take place out of Eskimo territory, but also American Indians are known to have used rattle sticks in their ceremonies. Furthermore, as we shall see, when the natives came back to trade they brought the pelts of inland animals back with them—something which Eskimos probably would not have done. And, if this weren't enough evidence, certain saga descriptions of the native weapons sound very much like weapons used by the Algonquin Indians, who were widely dispersed from the Great Lakes to the east coast and from Canada to Virginia.

The natives did not return that winter, and Karlsefni and his party settled down to a quiet, enjoyable life. They built their settlement on a hill facing the bay and permitted their livestock to graze freely.

In the springtime, though, the Indians returned in great numbers. The two sides went through the ceremony of showing each other rattling sticks and white shields, and then began to trade peacefully.

The Norsemen refused to barter their weapons, but offered red cloth which the Indians seemed to value. In exchange for a certain length of the cloth they demanded and received a marten, squirrel, or other such skin in perfect condition.

But the Indians were still eyeing those beautifully made European swords and spears. Eventually the inevitable happened; one native decided to steal one of the weapons he could not buy. A Norseman killed him and the rest of the Indians fled. (Another version has the natives frightened off by a bull, but a dispute over weapons is far more likely.)

Karlsefni was sure that the Skraelings would return—and this time prepared for war. He was right. Three weeks later a large fleet of skin-boats carried a war-party of Indians to the Norse encampment and the battle was on.

The Skraelings attacked the Vikings furiously, shouting their war cries and using war slings as well as bows and arrows. The Indians had another weapon as well, one which the Vikings had not seen before. It was a kind of catapult made from a long, flexible pole. The catapults sent great blue-black missiles flying into the rapidly crumbling ranks of Norsemen.

The women were watching this battle from a position of comparative safety. But when Eric's daughter, Freydis, saw the Vikings start to flee upriver, she became furious. Even though she was pregnant at the time, she came storming out of her house to scream and curse at the retreating backs of her countrymen.

"If only *I* had a weapon!" she cried. "I could fight better than any one of you!"

But the Viking men were too busy running away to listen to female curses.

Freydis followed them as best she could. Finding a dead Norseman in the forest, she took up his sword and prepared to defend herself against the Skraelings. As they came towards her, she ripped off her upper garments in a berserk fury and slapped herself with the sword.

It was not likely that the Indians had ever seen anything like this before. And they had no desire to see more of it. They took one look, spun about on their heels, ran back to their boats, and rowed away.

Just how true this story is, we cannot know. But it is certainly not impossible—or even improbable. Vikings did sometimes go completely berserk in the fury of battle (during pagan times, you may recall, Odin was the god of berserk fury) and the fact that Freydis was a woman did not make her any less a Viking. As for the Skraelings, they were faced with something entirely outside the range of their experience. This could well have made them run off in superstitious fear even though they were clearly winning the battle. Freydis, we are told, became the heroine of the now, no doubt, sheepish male Vikings.

As a result of this encounter the Norsemen were convinced that it would be foolish of them to stay on at Hop. Even though the country there had everything they might have wished for, they realized that it would be merely a matter of time before they were once again forced to battle against Indian tribes who vastly outnumbered them.

The Vikings sailed back north. When they arrived at Leifsbudir, they found that Thorhall the Hunter had not come back from his own explorations, so Karlsefni took a party to search for him. He had no success. Later it was learned that Thorhall's ship was caught by gales and driven back across the Atlantic. According to reports from traders, the men ended up in Ireland where they were taken captive and killed.

"Eric the Red's Saga" states that Thorvald Eriksson was killed by a native arrow while he helped hunt for Thorhall. It is hard to explain this contradiction. But perhaps there was another man named Thorvald with Karlsefni and the saga writer merely assumed that it was Thorvald Eriksson.

Those members of the expedition who still survived spent the winter at Leifsbudir. They had plenty of provisions now, and there was no danger of starvation. But a new sort of problem soon broke out. The unmarried men began to force their attentions on the married women, causing a great deal of personal strife within the camp. This may have been the final hardship which forced Karlsefni to admit even to himself that his attempt to plant a colony on the New World was doomed to failure. He and the others started back to Greenland in the spring.

Of the two ships that began the return voyage, only the one captained by Karlsefni made it. Bjarni Grimolfsson's vessel ran into trouble and sank on the way. Bjarni's knarr had only one smaller boat that was in good condition, and this boat had room for just half of those on board. Bjarni chose to go down with his ship, while the survivors managed to reach Ireland.

When Thorfinn Karlsefni's ship reached Greenland, he, his wife, and his infant son spent the winter at Brattahlid. Eventually, the family settled down on Karlsefni's farm in Iceland.

The last New World voyage mentioned in the sagas is recounted only in the "Greenlanders' Saga." This was the one led by Freydis —the illegitimate daughter of Eric the Red and the half-sister of Leif Eriksson.

We have just seen Freydis as a brave woman subject to sudden fits of fury. When such a fit came over her during the Indian attack at Hop, she was considered a heroine. But now she will appear in a less attractive light.

Since the Norse had such a masculine-oriented society, what was a woman doing in charge of such an expedition? Wouldn't it have been more reasonable for her husband, Thorvard of Gardar, to have been at least nominally in charge? Perhaps. But then perhaps Freydis Eriksdøttir was very much the leader in her family. Whatever the reason, Freydis was in charge from its inception to its end. The very idea of launching another expedition, in fact, seems to have come from her.

When Freydis learned that an Icelandic vessel owned by a pair of brothers named Helgi and Finnbogi was in Greenland for the winter, it was she, not Thorvard, who traveled from their home at Gardar to visit them. And it was she who brought up the possibility of a joint Vinland venture.

Freydis suggested terms. The brothers would take their own ship, she would take hers, and they would share equally with her in any profits. When the Icelanders agreed to this arrangement, Freydis went to Brattahlid and asked Leif for his Vinland houses. Leif came back with the same offer that he had made to Karlsefni. He would not give away Leifsbudir, but the expedition was welcome to make use of it.

With this out of the way, Freydis and the two brothers began making preparations to sail. According to their agreement, each ship would carry a total of thirty men and five women. But Freydis—to put it rather mildly—had a flexible attitude about such contracts. She hid five extra men aboard her own craft for numerical superiority if a fight between the groups should erupt.

From the moment the two ships reached Vinland, it was apparent that Freydis wanted to cause trouble. The ship bearing Helgi and Finnbogi landed there a short time before Freydis's, and the two brothers carried their possessions to Leifsbudir. As soon as Freydis landed, she ordered them to take their things out again.

"My brother loaned these houses to *me!*" she stated baldly, ignoring the Icelanders' objections that they understood it was to be share-and-share-alike.

Helgi and Finnbogi, muttering darkly that they were no match for Freydis in wickedness, beat a hasty retreat.

The Icelanders built their own camp some distance away from

Leifsbudir, while Freydis busied her crew with chopping lumber in order to make a cargo for her ship.

For a short time that winter there was a certain amount of contact between the camps. At the brothers' suggestion, the crews even competed together in various Viking games. But hostility was never far below the surface. Soon the games ceased and the two groups stayed apart from each other.

In the meantime, Freydis brooded. One way or another, she seemed determined to bring matters to a head. One morning she woke up very early and made her way to the Icelanders' house. Finnbogi was the only one there who was awake. Freydis stood silently in the doorway until he noticed her. Then she asked Finnbogi to come outside and talk to her. They sat down on a tree trunk which was lying next to the house.

"How do you like this country?" Freydis asked him.

Finnbogi replied that he liked it very much. What he did not like was the bitterness which had sprung up between them. He could see no reason for it.

Freydis agreed. It was senseless. But the reason she had come to see him, she explained, was that she wanted to leave Vinland. Finnbogi and his brother, however, had the larger ship. If they would be willing to trade vessels with her, she would go away.

That does not sound like a fair offer, and Finnbogi probably surprised Freydis when he accepted it. He and Helgi, he said, would do whatever would make her happy. This was apparently not the reply that Freydis was hoping for. As it turned out, she had no wish to leave Vinland. She wanted the brothers out of the way.

Freydis returned to her own house and climbed back into bed. Her husband blinked open his eyes and asked her why she was so cold and wet. She replied with a great show of indignation that she had just come back from calling on the brothers; she had asked them to exchange ships with her, but her request had made them so angry that they had abused and beaten her.

One cannot help wondering about Thorvard's first reaction to his wife's statement. Did he suspect that she was lying? Could he have really believed that any man would have been so bold as to strike the formidable Freydis? His response, in any event, apparently did not satisfy her, for she turned furiously on him and accused him of refusing to defend her honor. She could see now that she was far from her home in Greenland, she wailed. And if Thorvard did not play the man and take vengeance upon Finnbogi and Helgi, she would immediately divorce him.

This was a threat which had considerable force. Under Icelandic law, which also held good for Greenlanders, a member of either sex could obtain a divorce through a simple declaration. If a woman were later held justified in getting a divorce, she could claim one half of her former husband's estate.

Freydis kept taunting Thorvard until he finally ordered his men to rise and gather their weapons. Then he led them to the camp of the Icelanders.

No battle took place there. What took place was a slaughter. The brothers' men were still asleep, and the Greenlanders were able to tie them up and drag them outside almost before they knew what was happening. As each Icelander was dragged out, Freydis gave the order to have him killed.

Of all those who came to Vinland on the Icelandic ship, now only the five women were left. Freydis was anxious to be rid of them also. But the murder of women turned out to be too much even for Freydis's hardened crew. She could find no one who would carry out her orders.

She looked about angrily. "Give *me* an axe!" she cried.

A battle-axe was handed to her and she performed the grisly act herself. She and the others then returned to Leifsbudir.

"If fate should bring us back to Greenland again," she said before dismissing the company, "we shall say that those people decided to stay here. If any man dares to talk about what really took place, I shall have him killed."

They did return to Greenland. They sailed back in the larger ship and took a profitable cargo with them. Freydis—still nervous about the chance of someone's talking—was more than generous with the crew. She paid them handsomely and then went back to her farm with Thorvard.

For a while the scheme seemed to work. The former crew members kept their mouths shut. But very gradually, nasty rumors concerning the expedition began to circulate throughout the settlement.

How did these rumors begin? It isn't too hard to figure out. The affair had to have preyed on the consciences of some of the men at least. Perhaps they drank too much and hinted at dark doings to their friends. Or perhaps they talked in their sleep so that their wives overheard them.

Because Leif Eriksson was Freydis's brother, he probably would have been one of the last to hear the whispers. When the reports finally caught up to him, it is easy to imagine the shock and disbelief with which he greeted them. Freydis was a daughter of Eric's, after all. She was Leif's half-sister. She might be a little wild, but she could never be guilty of such a disgusting crime. . . . Or could she? Leif had to find out.

He began by seizing three of Freydis's men. He questioned them separately—and under torture—until there were no contradictions in their stories. When he was finished he knew everything that Freydis had done.

Now that he knew, however, what action was he going to take? No matter what she did, Freydis was still his sister. Leif acted in a very human manner—he hedged.

"I can't find the heart to punish Freydis as she deserves," he admitted finally. "But I will predict this much concerning her and her husband: Their descendants will never flourish."

From that time on, the saga tells us starkly, no one thought them worthy of anything but evil.

Freydis and Thorvard, in other words, were made to suffer social ostracism. Too mild a penalty for such horrible crimes? In one way, yes. But in a closely knit society such as Greenland's was, it might have been the harshest one of all.

More controversy has been generated by this account of Freydis's crimes than by any other tale in either the "Greenlanders' Saga" or "Eric the Red's Saga." While there are many experts who believe that these events probably did take place, others believe that the entire story is extremely unlikely, or even downright false.

Where does the truth lie? Before making up our minds, let's take a look at a few of the reasons that have been given for doubting the tale.

1) There is a great deal of quoted conversation in it—most of which is highly questionable. The only witness to the discussion between Freydis and Finnbogi, for instance, was Freydis herself. And in reporting it, she would have been careful to place the Icelander in a far worse light than he appears.

2) Freydis had gained her point peacefully. The Icelanders had agreed to exchange ships with her. She had no reason to murder anyone.

3) It goes against everything we know of Viking character to believe that Freydis's men would have obeyed her orders to murder the Icelanders when they were bound and defenseless.

4) Icelandic women were not meek and helpless creatures. They would not have waited like sheep to be slaughtered. They would certainly have defended themselves against Freydis, and since the odds were five to one in their favor would probably have ended up butchering her.

5) Freydis herself has a suspiciously mythic cast. Both her character and the fact that she was pregnant when she stopped the Indian attack in "Eric the Red's Saga" are reminiscent of too many primitive fertility goddesses who were also goddesses of death. One example of such a goddess in old Norse mythology is Freyja—whom Freydis was named after.

Of all these objections, the first seems to me the most serious. The word-for-word reproduction of conversations does cast a dubious light over them. The sagas, after all, were first written down one or two hundred years after the Vinland voyages. It would be a miracle if any of the quoted conversations were more than approximately correct.

The other four objections do not hold as much weight. The simple fact that Freydis had what she wanted need not have stopped her from committing murder. A glance at any daily newspaper should convince us that murderers often act from an inner disturbance. As to the idea that Vikings with their Teutonic tradition of blood feuds did not kill helpless men—that simply is not true. In an earlier episode we saw Thorvald Eriksson and his crew capture eight natives, kill them when they were prisoners, and then go guiltlessly to sleep. There is nothing improbable about Freydis's men following her orders to kill the Icelanders, especially if they were convinced that their mistress had been manhandled by them. The men did refuse to butcher the five women, but they must have bound them securely. They would certainly not have left the women free to brawl with Freydis. Finally, if Freydis's character does resemble that of certain primitive goddesses, the characters of all the gods and goddesses were at least partly drawn from people. There would have been something of the god Thor, for example, in any great warrior. And, naturally, there would have been something of a goddess of destruction in any destructive woman.

We have already seen a large number of instances in which the "Greenlanders' Saga" and "Eric the Red's Saga" flatly contradict each other. In every one of these cases, at least one of the versions has to be untrue. The sagas are blends of fact and fiction, history and romance. But how much fact and how much fiction? How much history and how much romance? No one can give an exact measurement. We can say, however, that there is probably a lot more historical truth in the sagas than in Homer's *Iliad*—which is a poetic account of a fanciful chapter in a real war. We can also say, on the other hand, that they are hardly as accurate as would be the reports of a responsible modern journalist. Having come to that conclusion about the sagas in general, there is no reason to think that it doesn't also hold for the story of Freydis.

If we have learned anything about the Vikings so far, it is that they were no more alike than are Americans of our own day. If frightful women such as Freydis were in their number, so were faithful wives like Gudrid and noble queens such as Aud the Deep-Minded. And could any two men be more unlike than volatile Eric the Red and cautious Bjarni Herjolfsson? Or the high-minded Leif Eriksson and the ineffectual Thorvard of Gardar? The extent of the Viking accomplishments—the fact that Norsemen did explore this continent and try to found colonies here—would not be half so impressive if they were a race of perfect, godlike beings.

IX.
Beyond Vinland

The Icelanders' sagas have given us detailed accounts of Viking men and women who braved unknown dangers to come to the New World. Combining information from the sagas with finds made by archaeologists, it is possible not only to suggest a likely location for Leif Eriksson's Vinland, but to make some educated guesses as to the whereabouts of other saga lands.

However, the saga voyages were not the only ones which the Norsemen made to this continent. Nor, for that matter, did the Vikings limit themselves to the areas we have discussed. There is substantial evidence, indeed, for at least one Norse journey to America that was undertaken many years after the saga period. This is the expedition which was in the charge of Eric Gnupsson, the first bishop of Greenland.

Bishop Eric Gnupsson was a native of Iceland. He was appointed to his Greenland post by King Sigurd I of Norway, who was also known as *Jorsalafar*, "Jerusalem-farer," after a crusade he made to the Holy Land. Practically nothing is known about the bishop's early life. The fact that he left for Greenland the year after Sigurd came back from Jerusalem might suggest that he was on this crusade with his king. But this is sheer speculation.

We can find Bishop Eric's name in the *Icelandic Annals*—a collection of manuscripts which recorded yearly events and were written down in the thirteenth century. There Bishop Eric states that he landed in Greenland in the year 1112. According to fourteenth-century evidence from Father Ivar Bardson, who was steward of the Greenland bishopric, Bishop Eric had his seat in the Western Settlement.

Why there? The Eastern Settlement was always more populous and more important than the Western. In the year 1124, Eric's successor, Bishop Arnald, made his seat in the Eastern Settlement. (This seat was at Gardar, incidentally—the same Gardar where Freydis and Thorvard once had their home.)

The Western Settlement was closer to America than was the Eastern Settlement, however. Thorfinn Karlsefni left from there. And the probable location of Bishop Eric's church was Sandnes—on property which had once belonged to Karlsefni. Is it not possible, therefore, that Bishop Eric's mission was not confined to Greenland but included the New World as well?

A reading of the *Icelandic Annals* for the year 1121 confirms that this was probably the case. For in that year, the *Annals* state, the bishop set out in search of Vinland. Since the *Annals* make no further mention of Bishop Eric, it has usually been assumed that he never made it back to Greenland. Chances were, most people thought, that he was either lost at sea or killed on the American continent. With the publication of the Vinland Map in 1965, however, a whole new light was shed on this matter.

In Chapter VI we saw that the map contains an explanatory legend which states in part that Bjarni and Leif discovered a new, fertile land which they named Vinland. This descriptive passage does not end there. It goes on to say that "Eric [Eric Gnupsson], legate of the Apostolic See and Bishop of Greenland and the neighboring regions, arrived in this truly vast and very rich land, in the name of Almighty God, in the last year of our most blessed father Paschal [Pope Paschal II, that is, who reigned from 1099 to 1118]." Bishop Eric remained in Vinland for a long period—"both summer and winter," the map states—before returning "northeastward toward Greenland." He then proceeded to another destination, probably Europe, at the instructions of his superiors in the church.

There is a discrepancy in dates here. The *Icelandic Annals* had the bishop leaving for Vinland in 1121, not arriving there in 1118. But this is a minor point. What's important is that the Vinland Map does confirm he left on such a journey, and claims that he not only got there safely but returned home again.

For what reason could this important churchman have gone to Vinland? His mission surely could not have been to preach to the Skraelings. That particular type of missionary urge did not develop in Europe until much later. The most logical explanation is that Bishop Eric paid a visit to one or more Norse colonies which must have still been in existence in the New World.

Once we accept that, the whole affair makes good sense. Eric was not only Bishop of Greenland, but, as the Vinland Map clearly states, in charge of the neighboring regions as well. At least one of those neighboring regions must have been located in North America. And, by having his official seat in Greenland's Western Settlement, Bishop Eric was well poised to journey there.

But what was there about that colony, or was it colonies, to induce the bishop to go there?

In order to merit the visit of a bishop, a colony would have had to be more than a mere outpost, simply a place for a Viking ship to dock and make small repairs while it picked up a cargo of timber. It would have been a real settlement with at least some degree of permanence. But if the Vikings remained in America after the saga period on any kind of permanent or even semipermanent basis, they must have left their mark. We are entitled, in other words, to ask for evidence.

We have already seen some evidence, of course. The very mention of Bishop Eric's voyage in both the *Icelandic Annals* and the Vinland Map is evidence. And we can add to this the fact that Vinland and Markland are mentioned in various European writings of the period. As late as 1347, in fact, the *Annals* describe a small Greenland ship which had sailed to Markland and was then storm-blown to Iceland.

All this comes under the heading of European evidence. Is there any physical evidence of later Viking visits on our own soil?

Though clear-cut enough, this question is impossible to answer with any degree of certainty. For while it is easy to find physical evidence on North America which some students of the Vikings claim is definitely Norse, there are other experts who claim just as forcefully that it is neither Norse nor evidence. All we can do here, therefore, is to take a look at some of these possible Viking "footprints" and see where they lead us.

The first clue we will examine is in many ways the most mysterious of all. If one were to write a book about it, indeed, it could be entitled "The Mystery of the Blond Eskimos."

Who are the blond Eskimos? What may be the earliest report on them comes from the year 1656, when a Dutch ship visited the shores of Baffin Island, which is located to the north of the great Labrador Peninsula and is separated from it by Hudson Strait.

According to an account of the voyage written by Cesar de Rochefort, the ship's company saw two very different types of natives there. The first type was made up of ordinary Eskimos—short in stature, dark in complexion, and with typically Mongoloid features. In addition, however, the crew saw people who were tall, light-complexioned, and fair-haired. Since then, reports of blond Eskimos with a Scandinavian look have come from many different sections of the Canadian north. In our own century, the Canadian-born Arctic explorer, Vilhjalmus Stefansson—a man who spent many years studying Eskimos and actually living with them—found a tribe of two hundred blond Eskimos above the Arctic Circle in central Canada, on the shores of Coronation Gulf.

How did these people originate? The most commonly held belief is that they are a result of an intermingling of Eskimos and whites. Post-Columbian whites, that is. The blending of the two groups is said to be increasing in the twentieth century.

But while this theory may explain certain of the blond Eskimos, it must be stretched somewhat to explain Stefansson's locating an extremely isolated group of them in the early days of the twentieth century. And it casts no light at all on the report of the seventeenth-century Dutch ship.

Is it not more likely, then, that these Scandinavian-looking people are actually descended from Norsemen?

But which Norsemen? That is the question we have to contend with. Their ancestors surely could not have been the Vikings who were mentioned in the sagas. All the saga expeditions left America with most of their members. The one small party—consisting of ten males under the leadership of Thorhall the Hunter—which may have remained here (or may have perished in Ireland as tradition has it, or may even have been lost at sea) cannot explain the persistence of the blond stock.

It seems more probable that the Scandinavian Eskimos are descended from later Norse colonists who may have been left on these shores as Viking power declined and Greenland sank into poverty. Perhaps the remnants of these people, vastly outnumbered by Indian and Eskimo tribes, were gradually pushed farther and farther to the north until they divided and scattered about the Canadian Arctic.

There is still another theory as to the possible identity of the Norse ancestors of the blond Eskimos. A clue to this theory lies in conditions on Greenland during the first half of the fourteenth century. We have already seen in Chapter V the sad and hopeless state that the once-proud island was reduced to by then. Half forgotten by Europe, under growing assault by migrating waves of Eskimos, the Norsemen on Greenland faced a bleak future.

Although life was not good any more on either of the two settlements, conditions on the smaller and more exposed Western Settlement were by far the more trying. Towards the end of the first half of the fourteenth century, the very survival of that settlement was in doubt.

About that time, Father Ivar Bardson, recently returned from Norway to his native Greenland and appointed steward of the bishopric in the Eastern Settlement, grew very concerned about the problems that the Norse in the west were having with the Skraelings. He decided to pay a visit to the Western Settlement in order to help drive the wretches out. The precise year of this visit is open to question; estimates vary from 1342 to 1350. But the journey was made.

When he arrived at his destination, Father Ivar was greeted only by ownerless horses and cattle. There was not a human being to be found. There were no dead bodies—no sign of plague or of a climactic war with the Eskimos. Just empty houses and wandering livestock.

There is little doubt that the Norsemen had left their homes of their own free will. Not only would there have been evidence of a struggle if they had been killed in battle, but the victorious Eskimos would have slaughtered the livestock for food. The only real question concerns where they might have gone.

To the Eastern Settlement? If that had been the case, Father Ivar would never have started on his journey. To Iceland or Norway? If they had gone there, the people of the Eastern Settlement—including Father Ivar—would have known about it. Their most probable destination, therefore, was North America.

This probability is reinforced by a synopsis of the *Icelandic Annals* for the year 1342 which was made in the seventeenth century by an Icelandic bishop after the original records were destroyed by fire.

The synopsis states that the people of Greenland gave up their Christian faith and turned to the people of America.

Of course, the original *Annals* would not have used the name "America." This was a later synopsis which was set down in 1637—seven years after the fateful fire. Vinland, or perhaps even the generalized term, the west, may have been the name used in the original, as the synopsis goes on to quote the *Annals* as having placed Greenland near the western lands of the world.

But the point here is the use of the word, "people." Which people of America did they turn to? We have only two choices: the Skraelings, and the earlier Norse colonists. Chances are the Greenlanders would not have turned to the Skraelings. They must have decided to give up their increasingly difficult existence on the Western Settlement and try to join their fellow Norsemen in "Vinland the Good."

The Norwegian-American historian and Viking expert, Hjalmar R. Holand, believes that it was the fourteenth-century Greenland emigrants who were the real ancestors of our blond Eskimos. There had to be at least a few hundred Greenlanders, enough to found a "new" people. They became known as the Tunnit or Tornit people—a mysterious lost people about whom there has been a good deal of puzzled speculation by modern scientists.

During their heyday, the Tunnit people lived on Newfoundland, Labrador, Baffin Island, and other places in the Canadian northeast. They were apparently larger in stature than either the Thule Eskimos who flourished at the same time or the present-day Eskimos who are descended from the people of the Thule culture. The Tunnit people lived in stone houses, were perhaps of a lighter complexion than the Thule folk, and at one time may have used the Thule people as slaves.

One theory concerning the Tunnit culture states that it is identical with still another Eskimo grouping, the Dorset people, who ap-

parently lived in the Canadian northeast before the Thule folk arrived. There are several difficulties with this explanation, however.
Not the least of these is that the Dorset culture was both earlier than
the Thule and considerably less developed in technology.

If the Tunnit folk were actually Norsemen and their descendants,
however, many things about this culture become clearer. Even in
their declining state, the Norse would have been more skilled in
weaponry and technical achievements than their Indian and Eskimo
neighbors. While it would not have been admirable for them to look
down on these neighbors and make slaves of them when they could,
it would have been quite natural. Since they were outnumbered,
however, they would have been forced out of territory after territory by the resentful Eskimo and Indian tribes.

This theory, therefore, is obviously "workable." But is it true?
Were the blond Eskimos actually descended from the Tunnit people? And were the Tunnit really Norse emigrants who left Greenland sometime between 1340 and 1350? This is something which we
cannot positively know.

We have good reason to state that Viking colonies were probably
on this continent after the saga period. We can say that it is very
likely that the missing people from the Western Settlement on
Greenland left to join them here. And we can also be fairly sure that
at least some of the blond Eskimos are descended from Norse stock.
But whether or not the Tunnit people are actually fourteenth-century emigrants from Greenland who were the ancestors of the blond
Eskimos is still a subject for speculation.

Another Viking "footprint"—one more controversial than the
blond Eskimos—is the famous "Stone Tower" in Newport, Rhode
Island.

This plain-looking structure has the distinction of being one of
the most argued-about buildings in North America. It is a round
tower which stands on eight round pillars that serve as supports for
arches. At their centers, the arches rise to about ten feet above the

The famous "Stone Tower" in Newport, Rhode Island. Some maintain that it was built by the Norsemen seven centuries ago. Others claim that it dates from about 1673.

ground. The tower itself has a diameter of about twenty-four feet on its outside. It is made of ordinary field stones held in position by good quality mortar. Its six-foot-thick walls are pierced by small windows and loopholes. It has a medieval appearance and looks almost like a miniature round fortress placed on circular stilts.

Who built this tower? What was its function? Here is where the controversy starts. Although many scholars believe that it was constructed by Norsemen in pre-Columbian times, the majority of experts insist that it was built in post-Columbian Colonial days—perhaps by the British, perhaps by the Dutch, or maybe even by the Portuguese.

The tower is usually referred to as "the old stone mill." There are those who believe that it was built by a man named Benedict Arnold—not the infamous Benedict Arnold, but an earlier namesake who was governor of the Newport Colony between 1633 and 1677. Governor Arnold not only owned the land that the tower is on, but in his will dated December 24, 1677, he mentioned that structure which he called his "stone-built windmill."

Whether or not the tower was ever used as a windmill, however, there are a good number of reasons to doubt that it was originally designed for that purpose. With its arches and columns, for one thing, it certainly does not resemble a typical windmill of the Colonial period. And, while the bottom of the tower is perfectly circular, the top is actually an oval—which would mean that the blades of the mill could not have efficiently changed direction as the wind changed.

There are other theories as to the tower's original function. It might have been designed as a watchtower by English colonists, or as a lighthouse, or been built by Portuguese pirates as a base from which to prey on shipping.

But there are basic flaws in all the theories. The tower, for example—which contains about one million pounds of stone and mortar and is supported by medieval-style arches—is an extremely complex structure for poor colonists (or pirates) to have built to serve a utilitarian function.

Most of those who believe that the tower was Norse in origin say that it served as the central part of a fourteenth-century (or earlier) church which may also have been used as a lighthouse, a fortress, and a watchtower.

The fact that the structure is circular is not a hindrance to the church theory. During the Middle Ages, many European churches were round in design. And there is a strong resemblance between the Newport Tower and certain fortified churches in Sweden. In rural Scandinavia, indeed, churches were often employed as local fortresses.

If the tower actually was designed to be a fortified church, it may have had a stone walk on the roof which would have been protected by a low wall or parapet to aid its defensive function.

Those who believe in the Norse fortified church theory have come up with several strong arguments, the strongest of which is that none of the other theories appears to make much sense. If we assume that the tower was built during the sixteenth or seventeenth century, in other words, we would be forced to believe that an expensive stone structure was put up in a pseudomedieval style merely in order to serve as a watchtower or a rather impractical windmill. All this is possible, of course, but not probable.

If the Norse had built the tower, on the other hand, it would have been designed to be the most important structure in their community: their place of worship, their community meeting-hall, their fortress in time of Indian attack, their lighthouse, and their watchtower. They would naturally have spared no expense or effort in its construction. And since they would have been living in the late Middle Ages, it goes without saying that they would have styled it in the medieval manner.

Probably the most important count against the Norse church theory is that even though the ground surrounding the tower was thoroughly excavated in 1948 and 1949, absolutely no Viking objects were discovered in the vicinity. The earliest finds dated from the Colonial period.

A possible explanation for this lies in the fact that previous excavations were made of the land around the tower. There were at least five of these that we know of and there were probably more. In the year 1848, for example, the then owner of the tower, Governor W. C. Gibbs, dug all the way down to the foundations. If any Norse objects were in the ground they may have been destroyed or taken as souvenirs by Governor Gibbs or others.

Let us assume for now that this structure really was designed as a Viking church. Which group of Norsemen might have built it?

Here, of course, we are drifting even further into the realm of educated guesswork. It might have been built by almost anyone who came here or stayed here after the saga period.

One theory has the tower being constructed as early as the 1120's by Bishop Eric Gnupsson. Another theory states that it was built in the middle of the fourteenth century by members of a Scandinavian expedition which was searching for the missing emigrants from Greenland's Western Settlement.

It is important to keep in mind, however, that all ideas about which Norsemen built the tower are thoroughly speculative, for it is still not certain that any Norsemen put it up.

The weight of expert opinion comes down on the side of the structure's probably being built during the Colonial period. Despite all the problems with that belief, the experts say, the difficulties connected with the Norse church theory are even greater.

But this dispute is far from settled. Each one of us is free to make up his or her own mind as to what really happened.

Of all the many arguments concerning the Vikings in America, the most bitter is the one surrounding the "Kensington Stone."

This is a flat stone, slightly under three feet in length, that has Old Norse runic writing chiseled into it. If it were found in Iceland or Norway there would be nothing extraordinary about it. There are many such runestones found in the former Viking territories. This particular stone, however, was found not in Europe, but on a farm located three miles from the small village of Kensington in Douglas County, Minnesota.

The Kensington Stone was discovered in August 1898 by a Swedish-born farmer named Olof Ohman. Ohman was clearing his land at the time, and he paid little attention to the slab of gray stone which was lodged under the roots of an aspen tree. But when his young son dusted off the rock with his cap, the boy noticed the odd-looking runic markings and called his father over to see them.

Mr. Ohman had no more idea of what the markings meant than

The Kensington Stone, discovered in 1898 by a Swedish farmer in Minnesota, has old Norse runic writing carved on it, alleged to be a message left by a band of Vikings in 1362.

did his son. Neighbors whom he invited to see the stone were also at a loss to explain them. It was only gradually that he and his friends noted a similarity between these marks and early Norse runes. Four months were to go by before a copy of the inscription was sent to the University of Minnesota.

The copy was seen there by Professor O. J. Breda, an expert in the field of Scandinavian languages. Although Professor Breda was not a specialist in runic writing as such, he was able to translate a large number of the marks on the stone. He gave out the opinion that the runes were probably not made by Norsemen, but had been carved into the stone as a joke.

By this time, the newspapers had gotten hold of the story and were starting to give it widespread publicity. Photos of the stone and copies of the markings were sent to several universities in Scandinavia, while the stone itself was sent off to experts in the United States.

We do not have all the replies from this enquiry. But from the ones we do have, the scholars were almost unanimous in deciding that the Minnesota runestone was the result of a hoax. There matters rested for a while. The man who had found the stone, Olof Ohman, was apparently disgusted by the affair and the publicity it generated. He left the stone lying face down and neglected on his property.

But in the summer of 1907, the Kensington Stone came to life again. Hjalmar R. Holand—the same Holand whose work we discussed in connection with the Tunnit people and the blond Eskimos—happened to be in Minnesota that summer in order to research a book he was writing on the history of the Scandinavian settlers in Minnesota. As Mr. Holand approached the area of Kensington, he heard more and more tales about the mysterious runestone. Farmer Ohman may have tried to put the subject out of his mind, but nearly everyone else in the region was talking about it. With his curiosity piqued, Holand made up his mind to visit the Ohman farm and see it for himself.

The farmer showed the stone to his visitor, and then offered to sell it to him as a souvenir for ten dollars. But when Mr. Holand replied that he could only afford half that amount, Ohman gave the object to him. He liked to help out young students, he said.

It was several months before Holand could find the time to study his "souvenir"—which was how he still thought of the stone. But once he began to inspect it seriously, he found himself becoming fascinated. Perhaps it was not a forgery after all, he speculated, but a genuine old Norse artifact.

Here is a translation of the runes which Mr. Holand made then and which I am quoting from his book, *Explorations in America Be-*

fore Columbus (Twayne Publishers, Inc., New York, 1956). The words in brackets were not marked on the stone.

[We are] 8 Goths [Swedes] and 22 Norwegians on [an] exploration journey from Vinland round about the west. We had camp by [a lake with] 2 Skerries one day's journey north from this stone. We were [out] and fished one day. After we came home [we] found ten of our men red with blood and dead. AVM [Ave Virgo Maria] save [us] from evil.

[We] have ten men by the sea to look after our ship 14 days-journeys from this island. [In the] year [of our Lord] 1362.

If this stone were all that it purported to be, it was of obvious historical importance. While there were many then who believed that the sagas were based on truth and that the Vikings had set foot on this continent, nobody dreamed that Norsemen might have penetrated as far into the interior as Minnesota.

Yet the more Holand studied it, the more he was convinced that the inscription on the stone was probably a true one, that a Viking expedition of twenty-two Norwegians and eight Swedes did reach what is now Kensington.

But how could this have been? There are no rivers leading from the American east coast to Minnesota; still the stone insists that the explorers had two small boats (the skerries) a day away from the stone-site and that their ship was fourteen days away.

Holand gradually worked out an elaborate theory to explain these facts. The expedition, he felt, was part of one which left Norway in 1355 under the leadership of a man named Paul Knutson. It was under orders of King Magnus VI, who ruled in both Sweden and Norway. Its assignment was to sail to Greenland and save the rapidly declining Christian faith there.

We still have a copy of the official letter, written in 1354, in which Paul Knutson received his commission. But there are no documents, royal or otherwise, to show what happened to it afterwards.

There is not even any actual proof that it ever sailed. Mr. Holand, however, and those who agree with him, believe that, given the religious atmosphere of the time, it is almost inconceivable that it did not depart for Greenland as the king had ordered.

If Paul Knutson did reach Greenland, he found the Western Settlement sadly deserted. What would he have done then? Would he have turned back to Norway? Or would he have acted as a true Christian and a loyal subject of his king and gone after the wayward Norsemen? Holand believes that he went after the Norsemen in the New World.

Assuming that Paul Knutson arrived on Greenland in 1355, he probably stayed there for a year or two—perhaps spending most of his time in the Eastern Settlement—before continuing his journey to North America.

If he had then made a direct crossing to Vinland and found that the Greenlanders were not there, he might have decided to explore northward up the Canadian coast, perhaps leading the search party himself or maybe staying at Vinland and appointing one of his lieutenants in charge of the further explorations. On the other hand, he may have made a northern crossing to the New World as Leif Eriksson had done. Either way, the members of the royal expedition would have eventually found themselves at the entrance to Hudson Strait.

It's important to remember now that, during the Viking era, North America was thought to be not a continent but a large island. Thus Paul Knutson, or whoever was in charge of the exploration party, would have believed that Hudson Strait was part of the ocean which encircled the "island." If they sailed into the strait and followed the shoreline, therefore, they should have been able to travel around the western "island" and examine it from every side.

A glance at a map will show what must have happened next. Hudson Strait leads directly into that enormous body of water known as Hudson Bay. If the ship headed south at the entrance to

Hudson Bay, it could have followed the shoreline in that direction for nearly one thousand miles before reaching the end of James Bay which lies between the present-day Canadian provinces of Ontario and Quebec. And for most or even all of that distance, the men must have thought that they were sailing on open sea and going around a monstrous island!

On the western bank of James Bay is the wide and inviting mouth of the Albany River where the Norsemen could have left their ship while they traveled upstream in the skerries. The Albany is a good-sized river which leads to a series of lakes near the Minnesota-Ontario border. From there, other bodies of water—plus short overland portages—would have led the men to the Kensington area.

What about the "14 days-journeys" that the runestone mentions? A day's journey was a kind of flexible Norse measure. The "14 days-journeys" would have meant that they had traveled about a thousand miles from where they left their ship.

There has been some evidence found to back up this theory. Implements which may have been made in the Viking era have been found in Minnesota—including three examples which were discovered near the spot where the ten men mentioned on the stone may have been killed. Chiseled holes in rocks which look startlingly like old Norse mooring holes—holes meant to secure the ringbolts of Viking boats—were located near the waterways which the Paul Knutson party may have used. The remains of an old wooden boat which may have been a Norse skerry were discovered less than six miles from where the stone was buried. But all this is supporting evidence. The major piece of evidence remains the Kensington Stone.

If the stone is genuine, the Vikings were in Minnesota. Even if the "Norse" boat turns out to have been built by nineteenth-century farmers, even if the "mooring holes" were drilled in the rocks to prepare them for blasting, even if the "Viking" implements were actually designed in British Hong Kong, a party of Norsemen still managed to reach what is now Minnesota. The only question would be how they did it. If the stone is a forgery, on the other hand, the supporting evidence must be studied with a very cynical eye.

The puzzle of the stone is still not solved.

Holand has devoted the better part of his life and what even his critics admit is a tremendous amount of physical and mental labor to proving its authenticity. Despite continuing attacks from recognized authorities, he has never once wavered in his belief. His research, furthermore, has won over a good many experts who were once on the other side.

But there is no getting around the fact that the overwhelming majority of the world's leading scholars on ancient Norse writings still believe that the Kensington Stone is a hoax.

If it was a hoax, who carried it out? This cannot be definitely known. Most of the experts seem to feel that it was either farmer Ohman or some other resident of the Kensington settlement who, in the last decade of the nineteenth century, decided to have some fun with the professors and then found his joke getting away from him.

Professor Erik Wahlgren, one of the foremost authorities in the field, sums up the case for the opposition in the conclusion of his book, *The Kensington Stone, a Mystery Solved* (University of Wisconsin Press, Madison, Wisconsin, 1958):

> *The style, spelling, grammar, numerals, and contents of the inscription on the stone forbid our thinking it medieval; but they are supremely appropriate to a writing in Minnesota dialect. . . . All available facts indicate that the inscription was carved in the 1890's, and probably in 1898.*

In my own opinion, the genuineness of the Kensington Stone remains an open question. Despite—or possibly because of—the great amounts of heat which have been generated on both sides, I do not believe that the final word on the runestone has been spoken.

I would suggest that anyone who is really interested in this puzzle read a couple of books—one on each side. You could begin, perhaps, with one of Mr. Holand's books or else an intriguing work written by Frederick J. Pohl, *Atlantic Crossings Before Columbus* (Norton, New York, 1961). Mr. Pohl has been associated with Holand and is also convinced of the stone's authenticity.

But once you have gotten the "pro" side of the argument, by all means turn to Professor Wahlgren's book. It may be that when you've finished looking into both sides of the question you'll be able to make up your own mind.

X.
The Viking Impact

The Vikings were here. They came to North America and they explored parts of it. They traded here and they settled here for a while. But granting all of that, what impact did the Norsemen actually make on this continent? On the surface, at least, very little. Their "footprints," as we have seen, are few.

Perhaps they were responsible for establishing a line of blond Eskimos. Perhaps they built a tower in present-day Rhode Island. Perhaps they carved a runestone in Minnesota. These things plus some rusting implements and the crumbling ruins of a few houses on Newfoundland are the very most they may have left behind them when they departed from these shores. As far as physically affecting the New World is concerned, the Vikings might almost not have come at all.

Yet it is foolish to say that the New World Vikings had no influence on Western history. They had some impact on the Europe of their day. And they have rather more on us now.

In their own time, the Viking influence on Europe was minor and basically confined to trade. We have already seen how timber, grapes, and/or berries from America found their way to Greenland and probably to Europe. More exotic items came from here as well.

The white falcon—the royal hunting bird of the Middle Ages—was probably captured on Baffin Island by Vikings and taken to Scandinavia where it was shipped to the most important courts in Europe. Polar bears from the American north were also taken to delight and astonish European royalty. Among still other items exported from this continent were turkeys and walrus-ivory.

In addition to whatever impact this trade had, the Viking discoveries had a certain intellectual influence on Europe. While Vinland, Markland, and the other western lands were certainly not the most popular subjects for dinner-table conversation during medieval times, they were written about and had to have been discussed. The New World was described on the Vinland Map, of course, and was mentioned in other European writings. The fame of Canada's Baffin Island apparently spread as far as Arabia where it seems to have been described by a thirteenth-century writer.

It is possible, however, that the most important pre-Columbian effect of the Viking explorations was that which it may have had on Christopher Columbus.

Columbus visited Iceland in 1477 and may have sailed some distance beyond it. While he was on Iceland, the future discoverer of "the Indies" must have heard local sailors speak of Greenland which had been in contact with the Icelanders until only recently.

Did he also hear something of the lands beyond Greenland? Did he hear of the saga tales or was he told anything of later voyages? Did he even see some Viking map—perhaps like the one which must have inspired the maker of the Vinland Map? These are the questions which plague us.

Shortly before Columbus reached Iceland, a Portuguese named João Vaz Cortereal may have been taken to the New World by a Scandinavian ship and crew. If this voyage had taken place, the ship would have set out from Norway in either 1472 or 1476 (estimates vary) and touched at Iceland on its way. Columbus surely would have heard about that. It is true that this voyage is as controversial as some of the others we have discussed. But even if it was never made, Columbus was on Iceland, and his curiosity about western lands may have been piqued there.

The Viking influence on us today is hardly tangible. Norsemen did not leave their language or culture or traditions in North or South America as did the Spanish, the English, the French, the Dutch, and even the post-Columbian Danes. Leif, Bjarni, and the other great Viking navigators are not honored by important place-names as are, for example, the great Italian navigators Christopher Columbus and Amerigo Vespucci.

But the emotional influence is great. Our blood cannot help being stirred by the saga tales of Vinland. We still stand in awe of the rugged band of merchant seamen who made their way to a New World in their efficient little open knarrs.

Yet they failed. If they had wanted to settle here and found a permanent colony—and they would hardly have brought their wives along if they did not want to settle here—they did fail. Either they did not remain, or those who may have remained lost their Norse identity to the Stone Age native population.

Why? As tough as they were, were they not tough enough? Were there simply too few Vikings to cope with the tribes of Indians and Eskimos that they found? Or was their own Norse culture too meager and not scientifically advanced enough to support a permanent colony? We may well ask these and other such questions, but the answers are not forthcoming. They are, and probably will remain, more mysteries to add to all the others concerning the mysterious Vikings.

But fail the Vikings did. We can say that much. Just as we can say that later on the Spaniards did not fail. They sailed far to the south to overwhelm the Indian people there (the Mayans, the Aztecs, the Incas, the Caribs, the Tainos), to enslave them and to destroy their ancient civilizations. And it was the Spaniards, led by that expatriate Italian, Christopher Columbus, who for better or worse bodily transferred European civilization to these shores.

And the Vikings . . . ?

We must be content to state that they wrote the introductory chapter in the book of European-American history. It was a brave chapter, from what we can read of it. And if its ending is poignant, poignancy at times seems the very stuff of history.

Index

About the Author

Morton J. Golding was born in New York City. After he received his B.A. and M.A. degrees from the University of Denver, he and his wife spent a year on the West Coast, returning to New York City to settle down. Mr. Golding has worked as a publicity writer and editor and now devotes his working life exclusively to writing books. He lives with his family in New Canaan, Connecticut.